# Options Trading Crash Course

*The Beginner's Guide to Make Money with Options Trading: Best Strategies for Make a Living from Passive Income and Quick Start to Your Financial Freedom*

**William Rogers and George Evans**

2

contained within this document, including, but not limited to, —
errors, omissions, or inaccuracies.

# Table of Contents

Gamma

Vega

Rho

Minor Greeks

What is Swing Trading?

Support and Resistance

Trade with the Trend

Swing Trading Options

Going Long on a Stock

Shorting Stock Using Put options

Tools to Spot Trend Reversals

Chart Patterns That Indicate Trend Reversals

Candlestick Charts

Moving Averages

Relative Strength Indicator

Bollinger Bands

Removing Direction from the Trade

Central Goal of the Iron Condor

Iron Condors are Income Strategies

The Lower Legs

The Other Legs

The Complete Iron Condor as a Single Trade

The Iron Condor Relies on Time Decay

The Iron Butterfly

# Introduction

Congratulations on purchasing the *Options Trading Crash Course,* and thank you for doing so.

The concept of options trading strikes most investors as obscure and even dangerous and risky. However, as we are going to learn in these pages, investing and trading in options is actually a smart and effective way to make money and build wealth. We'll begin the book by explaining what options are and how they work. There are different types of options and multiple strategies used to trade options, and we'll learn about the most popular that are available. You'll learn how to go about trading options and how to work with your broker.

The goal of this book is to demystify options trading. When you learn what they are and why they exist, the shroud of mystery that surrounds these supposedly exotic financial instruments will vanish. You'll find out that options trading, when done with care, is actually a straightforward way to engage with the financial markets. By the end of this book, you'll be able to clearly define a call and a put, an iron condor, a spread, and even the so-called "Greeks".

We'll also learn about the psychology and mindset that are necessary for successful options trading. You'll come to understand how options trading differs from stock trading and investment, both in mindset and goals and techniques. You'll also learn about the most serious mistakes that beginners make when trading options and how to avoid them. You'll also learn how to use options in order to generate regular income.

Until recently, options trading has only been available to financial insiders. The development of technology associated with the markets has changed all that, and now anyone can trade options, and you only need a few hundred dollars to get started. With all the user-friendly trading platforms that are now available through the internet and on mobile, the only obstacle is that most investors don't understand options. This book will help to remove that obstacle so that you can join those earning profits and income from options trading.

So, thank you for choosing this book. There are a number of various titles on this topic out there. So, your choice of this book is certainly motivating. We hope that you will get the most out of this book as great care has been taken in making sure that it is both useful and informative.

10

# Chapter 1: An Introduction to Options Trading

The first step to consider when engaging in options trading is to have a clear and accurate understanding of what an option actually is. Unfortunately, one of the things that is lacking in our society is a good financial education. Most people barely understand what the stock market is and how it operates, and options are a level above even that. In this chapter, we are going to lay a foundation for the rest of the book by helping you to understand what options are, why they exist, and what the different types and characteristics of options are. Then we will go into detail in the rest of the book so that you'll learn everything you need to learn in order to actually be able to trade options with success. Remember that all forms of investing and trading carry financial risk, and not everyone who invests or trades on the markets is going to succeed.

## What Is an Option?

Options are not restricted to the stock market. The name option gives us a clue as to what these financial instruments are, however. An options contract is one which enables the buyer to have the *option* to do something. Options contracts can exist in any context where you are interested in buying something. The proverbial example that is used is the option to buy a new home.

Let's say that Jane is moving to her new job in Houston, Texas. She is interested in buying a new home in a good neighborhood that is reasonably close to her job. She has two kids, so she's also interested in buying a home in an area with a low crime rate and good schools.

She finds out that there is a new housing development near her job. She also finds out that it will take about 4 months to have a home ready for her to move in. Because of the high demand in the area, home prices are changing rapidly. She'd like to lock in a price for a home but wants to look around in the meantime. How can she do that? The answer is she can enter into an options contract with the developer.

The type of homes that Jane is interested in are currently going for $350,000. Jane tells the developer she is willing to buy a house at this price, but she needs 120 days to decide. The developer knows that prices are rapidly increasing, but to make a deal. He offers the possibility for Jane to lock in a lot and home for $360,000. She must buy the home on or before the date the contract expires 120 days from the date, she signs it. If she fails to close by that time, the contract expires, and the developer is free to sell the lot to someone else at market prices.

Jane is not taking too much risk because she is not forced to buy the home; she has the option. If prices end up dropping, she can simply let the option contract expire. If prices stay about the same or keep rising, and she doesn't find another home she is interested in, Jane can go ahead and exercise her rights under the contract and buy the house for $360,000. This is true even if the price of new homes in the area has jumped to $400,000 at the time the contract expires. So, by locking in a price, Jane may have put herself in a position where she could save a significant amount of money yet get the home (investment) that she wanted.

While laws may vary based upon the given specific contract type, though generally speaking, the contracts themselves can be bought and sold. The contract itself becomes valuable because of the *underlying* asset (in this case, the home), and the ability to buy that asset at the fixed price. In an environment of rising prices, this can provide a big advantage to buyers. In many cases, the buyers won't go through with the contract. Actually, executing the contract is called *exercising* the contract. Of course, if home prices in the area were to rise to $400,000, it would be worth it to exercise this options contract.

Jane may not want to do so. Maybe she found a different home more to her liking. However, since the contract has obvious value, she could sell it to someone else. Ever since financial instruments were invented, secondary markets were created soon afterward, where people traded them. Options are no exception.

Since an option derives its value from an underlying asset that is not directly traded or even owned by the person who buys the option, it is called a *derivative*. The media often talks about derivatives as if they are extremely exotic and complex, but it is really nothing more than that. A derivative is a financial instrument or contract that derives its value from an underlying asset.

## Options on Stocks

The basic concepts of options that we described above apply to options on stocks. Since we now understand those basic concepts, let's define the specifics when it comes to options contracts on stocks. It turns out that options contracts on stocks are slightly more complicated than what we've described so far, but it's not horribly complicated if you take it step-by-step.

The first thing to note is the underlying. As far as options on stocks are concerned, its corresponding asset is 10 shares of a specific stock. That stock is a stock of a publicly-traded company on a major stock exchange. Options on stocks also include index funds. So, you can trade options on Apple, Facebook, or Boeing. You can also trade options on SPY, DIA, and QQQ, which are exchange-traded funds for the most significant stock markets such as the Dow Jones Industrial Average, the Standard & Poors 500, and NASDAQ 100, respectively.

For example, using a home purchase, we only talked about the option for someone to buy the home – we never considered having the option to sell a home. But with stocks, both concepts are equally important. The most basic concept is imagining having an option that would give you the possibility of purchasing those 10 shares of a given stock at a pre-determined sale point on or prior to the expiration date of the contract. This kind of deal is known as a *call option.*

You can see that in a market of rising prices, a call option favors the buyer. The potential buyer can lock in a price, and if they choose to do so, if the price per share actually rises by a significant amount (and by significant we mean significant enough to earn a profit if you turned around and sold the shares on the market), the buyer can buy shares at a discount.

In an environment of rising prices, since the option contract would give buyers such an advantage, that means the contract itself becomes more valuable. So, with everything else remaining equal, the price of said contact will be going up in a market of rising prices. People will be bidding up the price as more investors excitedly want to get their hands on the option.

There are going to be two types of buyers in the marketplace. Some buyers are really interested in getting a hold of the stock at a discount price. Others are simply hoping or anticipating that prices are going to continue rising, and so they anticipate that the price of the option is going to be higher in the future. In other words, they want to buy the option, and then turn around and sell it for a higher price a few days or weeks later at a higher price, so they can make a profit *from the option contract itself.*

When we are talking about anticipating making a profit from future changes in price, this is called speculating. The term speculating is associated with *trading,* which can be defined as short term purchase and sale of a financial asset with the sole intent of generating profits. It is important to keep this concept distinct from *investing.* The first difference between trading and investing in the time frame. Trading is generally done on short-term time frames of one year or less. In contrast, investing generally means five years or more. Investing is a long-term commitment to something you believe in.

Of course, investors hope that their assets are going to increase in value as well. Otherwise, they wouldn't invest. But they are in it for the long haul and are not going to be getting rid of their assets soon after they acquire them. The reasons for investing often go beyond simple profit. Investors may be passionate about the companies they invest in and the products they offer or believe that the companies they invest in represent the future of the economy. They may also take a broad view, and invest in index funds, based on the idea that the economy will grow with time.

It is crucial to have a clear understanding of the difference that lies between trading and investing, and understanding what "speculating" is, as an options trader. As we'll see later, you might have to express the fact that you understand the difference as an options trader to satisfy regulators.

## Put options

Now let's turn our attention to the other major type of option on the equities market. The option we are going to be discussing is known as a "put option". This kind of contract entitles the buyer to acquire a set quantity of stock at a pre-determined sale point. That might appear to you as somewhat bizarre at first, so why would anyone want to do that? The answer is that put options are valuable to buyers in a market of declining prices. If the stock is dropping significantly below the fixed price agreed upon in the options contract, then it makes sense to either do one of the following. If you already own the shares, maybe you purchased them at a much higher price, and you want to limit your losses. In that case, a put option allows you to cut your losses at a given price point that may be significantly above the market valuation. You don't have to worry if the market price keeps dropping, you can sell your shares at a price agreed to in the contract at any time before it expires. So, in this case, a put option can be a form of insurance for a buyer that has invested in a lot of shares.

It's also possible for speculators to profit. The first case is where you really want to sell the stock. To do this, you wait until the stock price drops low enough so that making a move on the option would be profitable. So, you buy the 100 shares and then sell them to exercise your rights under the option. Of course, the way this would work is you would sell them to the originator of the options contract, who is obligated to honor the contract and buy the shares.

But just like call options, if prices are moving favorably, the value of put options themselves is going to be increasing. This means that if stock prices are dropping, the price of put options will be rising, all other things being equal. That provides many opportunities for traders to earn profits. You buy the put options when they are at a relatively high pricing point, and then you sell them when the stock price drops, for a profit. The buyer may be a speculator who is simply interested in trying to sell the option at a later date for a profit, or it may be someone who owns the shares and wants that insurance that we talked about earlier.

## Selling Options and Options Strategies

Of course, there are all these options on the market to buy, but who sells them in the first place? Lots of people sell options. Options are not issued by the companies themselves, so in other words, Facebook does not issue options on its own stock. However, in some cases, big institutional traders might sell options. We say that the creator of an options contract *writes* the contract. Another way to put it is to say that they *sell to open*. As it turns out, not only can you buy options as an individual trader, you can sell to open options contracts as well.

This is a more advanced way to deal with options, so we will be talking about this later in the book after we've gotten a thorough understanding of trading options. Generally speaking, selling to open is an income strategy. So, people sell to open options and get paid when someone buys the option they are selling. They hope that this is the end of it (see below). Traders, on the other hand, will buy to open their positions, and then hope to make profits and trade away the option before it loses value. Trading is significantly riskier than selling options for income.

There are many strategies used when selling options. This can be used to reduced risk, but many experienced options traders sell what are called "naked" options. This is just straight up selling of options contracts to earn income. Of course, there is a risk with a naked option that you'll have to buy or sell the shares of stock. Since we are talking about 100 shares at a time (a single options contract covers 100 shares of stock), that can be a non-trivial amount of cash that you need to have on hand. It is also possible to sell options that are backed by either the full amount of cash or shares of stock that you already own. We will be talking more about this later.

Selling options can also be used in complex strategies in combination with buying options at the same time. This is done in multiple ways in order to minimize risk. These types of strategies also allow you to play different kinds of market situations. For example, many times, the stock doesn't go up or down very much. Instead, it stays trapped – often for very long periods – within a narrow range of prices. In that case, we say that the stock is "ranging". There are options strategies that allow you to earn profits when the price of a stock doesn't change very much. That may seem mysterious right now, but later in the book, you'll learn exactly how that works. An astute observer will note that this is a way to earn money that simply isn't possible investing in or trading stocks. This illustrates the explosive power that options provide.

Another strategy that can be used with options is you can sell options while limiting risks. These types of strategies are known as "spreads". Moreover, either selling naked options or trading in spreads, you can set up trades that make profit either when the stock price rises, or when it falls. This is another illustration of the power that options provide to traders, that is not available to stock traders. You might note that stock traders can "short" a stock to earn profits from market declines, however, to do that you have to be a major player with a large account. For most individual traders, shorting stock is going to be out of reach.

There are also strategies that can be used to earn profits if the stock goes up a large amount very quickly, or if it drops a large amount very quickly. So, you can make a profit no matter which way the stock moves, but there has to be a situation where there is going to be a large movement in stock price. A common time that this type of strategy is used is when there is an earnings call for a large company.

We are going to discuss all the details behind options trading strategies throughout the book so that you can become an expert in short order. You'll also learn all the meaning behind all the jargon behind these strategies that are probably floating around on the internet. For now, just be aware that there are many different ways that you can trade options as a buyer and a seller in order to earn money, and that you can do it under any condition that the market happens to be in. This type of flexibility is something that stock traders and investors, even "day traders", simply don't have access to.

# Chapter 2: Options Basic Definitions

In the last chapter, we went over the basic concept of an options contract as a derivative that gets its value from some underlying financial asset. In this chapter and from now on, we will turn our attention strictly to options on stocks (and index funds trading as stocks). The purpose of this chapter is to define and explain all the basic properties of options and the basic terminology.

## Strike Price

For a call option, there is a fixed price that is a part of the contract, which allows the buyer to purchase any amount of stock corresponding to a specific company at a pre-determined. The set price contained in the contract can be termed as the "strike price". The strike price of this kind of contract is one of its most important characteristics, and when you go to look for options to trade, you are going to see them listed in order by strike price. So, who do you purchase the shares from? You would buy the shares from the seller of the options contract. In the event they were not able to fulfill their end of the deal, the broker would step in and do it for them (with consequences to the seller). The strike price must be used independently of the stock's current market valuation. As such, if there is a strike price of $50, but the stock's current market valuation has risen to $350 per share, it's not relevant. The seller of the call option would still be required by law to sell you 100 shares at $50 a share.

The concept is the same for put options. In this case, the strike price of this kind of contract entitles the holder to trade a specific amount of a stock. As in the case of call options, you would be selling the shares to the originator of the put option. They would be legally bound to buy the shares of the stock whose valuation has been determined by the seller regardless of its perceived current market valuation.

## Expiration Date

Next, we come to the other crucial piece of information, which is the date of the expiration date of the contract itself. Generally speaking, the most common way in which options can be traded are listed is first by expiration date. When you select a given expiration date, you will then see options listed by strike price. On some platforms, options are all listed on the same page but grouped according to type. So, you will see all the call options listed at the top, and then this will be followed by the put options. In other cases, you will see a tab that lets you move back and forth between call and put options for the same expiration date.

As we will see, the expiration date is very important for many reasons. As this critical deadline approaches, if the contract does not have an appropriate valuation with regard to stock's current market valuation, it's going to be rapidly losing value. Let's get some insight into this with this sample situation. Let's assume that you are looking to purchase a contract for a call option that has a current strike valuation of $10. With this trade, you are looking to make a profit when its price increases. As such, the option has the greatest value when its current market valuation exceeds $10. Consequently, you profit more, the higher the price gets. Now, let's assume that its current market valuation falls to $7 instead. Then that call option simply isn't worth anything. People can just buy shares for $7, so why would anyone enter into a contract that required them to buy shares at $10 a share? Of course, they wouldn't do that. The longer you have remaining on the deal, the greater the value it has. If there are three months left on the contract, then it might still have a little value, because there would be a chance that the stock could move significantly in that time frame. But, if there are only three days left on the contract, the chances of the stock increasing from $7 to above $10 are pretty much nil (unless an earnings call is coming up and it turns out to be unexpectedly rosy), so the option will be rapidly losing value.

The expiration date is also important because when an option expires, it may be in a position where it can be exercised. Of course, there are as many approaches to this situation as there are unique individuals. Some people are small traders and simply don't want to buy or sell stock, and they may not have the capital to do so even if they wanted to. Remember, we are talking about 100 shares for each options contract.

On the other hand, others may be looking to buy and sell the shares. So, they may want to exercise the option when it expires, or even beforehand. If you are not able to buy and sell shares, you'll probably want to get out of the option before it expires to avoid this situation. In other words, you'll want to get whatever profits you can from selling the option. So, you want to sell it prior to the expiration date.

The expiration date is closely associated with a concept called time decay (and time value), so let's go ahead and discuss that.

## Time Decay

Time decay is an important factor to consider when trading options. For buyers, time decay works against them. For options sellers (that is people who sell to open options contracts), time decay works in their favor.

Earlier, we touched on the basic idea of time decay. When there is a long time until the option expires, there is a higher probability that the price of the option can move in one direction or the other. That means that the market price of the shares can move in such a way as to make the option profitable. On the other hand, as time passes, that probability that this is going to happen decreases. In fact, each day, that probability drops. This is known as time decay.

Time decay actually refers to a drop in the price of the option on the options market. Options pricing is complicated and described by mathematical formulas, and a part of that is value that comes from the time remaining until the option expires. This value is called time value, and time value translates into real dollars and cents. Again, as we will see, there are several elements that influence the valuation of an options contract, so it might so happen that an option is gaining overall value even as it loses time value. Down below, we'll discuss that a little bit more. In other cases, time value will be dropping rapidly, and the price of the option is going to be dropping with it.

Time value is also known as extrinsic value. Time value is extrinsic because it only relates to the time remaining on the options contract. We are simplifying a little bit, but this is generally the way to think of it. So, it's not derived from the underlying market valuation for this stock. Pricing of the option that comes from the underlying stock is known as intrinsic value.

# Options Chain

The list in which options for stocks and even index funds that are up for sale is known as the options chain. Every option has a ticker, although many modern platforms don't bother with that anymore since options information can be displayed in a user-friendly manner using computer and mobile technology. The options ticker includes information on the option such as which underlying stock the option is for, the expiration date, type of option, and the strike price. It might look something like this:

AMZN200103C1530000

The first part of the options ticker is the stock ticker of the underlying stock or index fund for the option. This is followed by the expiration date, which is given in a 2-digit year, month, and day format. So here we see:

200103

This means January 3, 2020. So, the format is YYMMDD. Following this, we see a single letter representing the type of option. In the case of AMZN200103C1530000, since we see a C in this position, that means that we are dealing with a call option. Had it been a put option, we'd see AMZN200103P1530000.

The last part pertaining to the contract is its strike price. This valuation (strike price) will have three decimal places and leading zeros if the strike price uses up all the digits. In other words, 1530000 represents a strike price of $1,530. If the strike price had been $851, the ticker would look like this:

AMZN200103C0851000

Tickers are displayed grouped by expiration date, with calls first, followed by put options, but probably with the ability to switch between them.

| | | | | | yahoo! finance | | Search for news, symbols or companies | | | | 🔍 | | | |

| | Finance Home | Watchlists | My Portfolio | Screeners | Premium 🔒 | | Markets | Industries | Personal Finance | | Videos |
|---|---|---|---|---|---|---|---|---|---|---|---|
| AMZN200103C01835000 | 2019-12-31 3:59PM EST | 1,835.00 | 19.75 | 18.45 | 20.15 | -2.02 | -9.28% | 477 | 0 | 16.53% |
| AMZN200103C01837500 | 2019-12-31 3:59PM EST | 1,837.50 | 17.70 | 16.65 | 18.15 | -2.30 | -11.50% | 614 | 0 | 15.97% |
| AMZN200103C01840000 | 2019-12-31 3:58PM EST | 1,840.00 | 16.57 | 15.45 | 16.80 | -2.72 | -14.10% | 3,457 | 0 | 16.22% |
| AMZN200103C01842500 | 2019-12-31 3:59PM EST | 1,842.50 | 15.20 | 14.05 | 15.50 | -3.10 | -16.94% | 1,228 | 0 | 16.42% |
| AMZN200103C01845000 | 2019-12-31 3:59PM EST | 1,845.00 | 13.75 | 13.50 | 14.10 | -2.74 | -16.62% | 1,840 | 0 | 16.38% |
| AMZN200103C01847500 | 2019-12-31 3:59PM EST | 1,847.50 | 12.70 | 11.60 | 12.85 | -2.47 | -16.28% | 967 | 0 | 16.43% |
| AMZN200103C01850000 | 2019-12-31 3:59PM EST | 1,850.00 | 11.55 | 11.05 | 11.75 | -2.89 | -20.01% | 4,883 | 0 | 16.58% |
| AMZN200103C01852500 | 2019-12-31 3:59PM EST | 1,852.50 | 10.40 | 9.55 | 10.60 | -2.45 | -19.07% | 675 | 0 | 16.56% |
| AMZN200103C01855000 | 2019-12-31 3:59PM EST | 1,855.00 | 9.40 | 8.45 | 9.40 | -2.90 | -23.58% | 1,197 | 0 | 16.37% |
| AMZN200103C01857500 | 2019-12-31 3:58PM EST | 1,857.50 | 8.30 | 8.00 | 8.55 | -2.90 | -25.89% | 918 | 0 | 16.55% |
| AMZN200103C01860000 | 2019-12-31 3:59PM EST | 1,860.00 | 7.50 | 7.00 | 7.80 | -3.07 | -29.04% | 2,591 | 0 | 16.77% |
| AMZN200103C01862500 | 2019-12-31 3:59PM EST | 1,862.50 | 6.90 | 6.60 | 7.05 | -2.80 | -28.87% | 446 | 0 | 16.90% |
| AMZN200103C01865000 | 2019-12-31 3:59PM EST | 1,865.00 | 6.15 | 5.75 | 6.35 | -2.68 | -30.35% | 836 | 0 | 17.01% |
| AMZN200103C01867500 | 2019-12-31 3:59PM EST | 1,867.50 | 5.56 | 5.15 | 5.65 | -2.60 | -31.86% | 634 | 0 | 17.04% |
| AMZN200103C01870000 | 2019-12-31 3:59PM EST | 1,870.00 | 5.05 | 4.85 | 5.15 | -2.52 | -33.29% | 1,813 | 0 | 17.28% |
| AMZN200103C01872500 | 2019-12-31 3:59PM EST | 1,872.50 | 4.60 | 4.20 | 4.70 | -2.27 | -33.04% | 271 | 0 | 17.54% |
| AMZN200103C01875000 | 2019-12-31 3:59PM EST | 1,875.00 | 4.12 | 3.65 | 4.25 | -2.23 | -35.12% | 1,029 | 0 | 17.72% |
| AMZN200103C01877500 | 2019-12-31 3:59PM EST | 1,877.50 | 3.75 | 3.40 | 3.80 | -2.09 | -35.79% | 351 | 0 | 17.83% |

*The options chain for Amazon.*

As we said, many platforms no longer use the tickers and simply display the options by strike price in a user-friendly, readable format. Below, we see the contrast between the traditional display used by Yahoo Finance, and a newer user-friendly display used by the mobile trading platform Robin Hood:

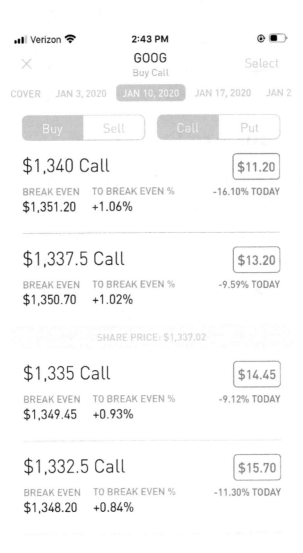

Here we see that you can simply click on a date at the top of the screen. For that date, we are able to move between call and put options with a single tap, and also between the purchase and sale. The options are listed in rows, going from highest strike price to lowest one, with the prevailing market valuation noted on the screen. The actual price of this contract is displayed on the right side of the screen, along with some other information.

## How Options Are Priced

Options prices are quoted on a per-share basis. For the vast majority of options contracts, there are 100 underlying shares of stock. So, the quoted price is for one share, but to buy a single options contract, you'll be doing it for all 100 shares. Fractional purchases of options are not allowed. So, if you see the price of an option quoted as $2, that means to buy the option, you actually have to pay $200.

As you can see, some options are quite expensive, but the price varies considerably. In the example using Google above, the last option at the bottom has a price of $15.70. That means to actually buy this option. You must pay $1,570. Of course, looking at it another way, you could sell the option for $1,570, and that might clue you in as to why people are interested in selling options contracts. More on that later. Next, we are going to cover some industry jargon that refers to the relationship between the market valuation of the individual stock and its strike price.

## In the Money

An option can be said to be *in the money* when it would be prudent to exercise it. In doing so, the transaction would generate a profit. As such, the term "in the money" means that the current valuation of a call options contract is greater than the current market price of the shares. The same can be said about a put options contract when its share price is below the valuation of the contract itself. But in reality, we need to take into account the price paid for the option. So, let's look at a more formal and more accurate definition.

In the case of a call option, this implies the market valuation of the shares is higher than its strike price in addition to the *breakeven* (note that in the options trading world, breakeven is two separate words). The breakeven price is simply the price paid to enter into the options contract. So, if the strike price of a call option is $100, and you buy that option for $1 (per share – so total of $100), the breakeven is $100 + $1 = $101. What this tells you is that its market valuation must increase to $101 in order for the option to be worth exercising.

For put options, remember that profit is earned from declining share prices. So, to get the breakeven price of a put option, you subtract the price per share spent on the option from the valuation of the contract. So, if we have a put contract containing a $90 valuation that costs $0.80, then the breakeven price would be $90 - $0.80 = $89.20.

Also, if the valuation of the stock drops below the strike valuation of a put contract minus the value paid, in other words, share valuation has fallen beneath the breakeven point. This is when the contract is said to be in the money.

## At the Money

The term "at the money" means that the valuation of the shares is the same as the market valuation of the contract. We use the same definition for both call and put options. Keep in mind that in reality, you can basically consider an option as "at the money" when the valuation of the shares goes below its breakeven point, but at or above the market valuation for the contract in questions. For a put option, you would for practical purposes consider an option at the money in the event the valuation of the shares was over the breakeven point but below the strike valuation. An at the money option isn't really anything special, other than being close to the possibility of going in the money at some point. The more time remaining until the option expires, the more useful an at the money option is. If you have a strong reason to believe that a stock is going to move one way or the other, using the money options could be a lower-cost way to get into the trade.

## Out of the Money

An out of the money option is one that is in a position relative to the market price of the stock such that it would not be worth exercising. For a call option, it will be out of the money when the strike price is above the strike price. Using the logic of the last section, in practice, you could consider it to be out of the money when it is above the stock price plus the break-even, but that is really a distinction without a difference when the option expires. An out of the money option will expire "worthless". Let's use a simple example to see why.

Remember the point of a call option. The purpose of a call option is to give someone the right to buy 100 shares of stock at a discount. So, let's say we buy a call option on some stock with a strike price that is $200 a share. Our speculation that the price of the stock was going to rise turns out wrong, and instead of going up, the price of the shares drops. As the option is nearing the expiration date, the price of the shares drops to $195 a share.

You can ask yourself if it would be worth exercising an option that gave you the right to buy 100 shares at $200 a share. Of course, it wouldn't be worth doing this. So, nobody is going to do it, and fewer people will want to buy the option from you if you wanted to get rid of it by trading it. Of course, some people will still buy it, as some naïve traders (and there are a lot of them – but we are educating our dear readers) will buy out of the money options because they are cheap, and there is always the "hope" that the stock price will reverse and gain value.

In most cases, that hope is not realistic, so it is not advisable to buy out of the money options, except in a narrow situation that we will discuss in chapter 4.

Now let's turn our attention to put options. Since put options earn profit when the stock price drops, that means a put option is going to be out of the money if the strike price of the option is lower than the share price of the stock.

## Open Interest

When you are looking for options to trade, there are other factors besides the strike price and expiration date that you should be looking at. One of these is called open interest. Open interest is the number of contracts that are on the market for a given stock, strike price, and expiration date. Some options are really popular, and you will see open interest in the tens of thousands. Others are not so popular – but could still be worth trading. A good rule of thumb that is used by professional options traders is you shouldn't get into options trades if the open interest is lower than 100.

There is a simple reason for this. You might need to find a buyer very quickly for an options contract to get out of a trade. This can happen when the price is moving in a favorable direction and when it's moving in a bad direction. The reason is that the relationship of the price of an option to the underlying shares is such that price movements of the stock are magnified in price movements of the option. Remember that there are 100 underlying shares of the option. So, a $1 price movement in the share price could, in theory, have up to 100 times the impact on the price of the option. We will discuss the actual values when we discuss the Greeks, but for in the money options, the relationship will be $0.50 to $1 per share, meaning that the price of the option can rise or fall $50 to $100 for in response to a $1 shift in the price of the underlying stock.

For at the money options, the relationship is $0.50 per share, so even at the money (or close thereto) options are massively impacted by price shifts in the underlying stock. It is this magnifying effect that makes options so attractive to many traders. In fact, although its operating at a lower level, large price shifts can even have a large impact on the prices of out of the money options, even a few days before expiration.

The bottom line here is that you can gain or lose money very quickly. When you've made a large profit, you're going to want to sell your options to someone else before the price moves in the opposite direction, and you end up losing money as fast as you've made it. These cuts both ways. Sometimes an option is destined to simply lose a lot of value. If you find yourself in a losing trade, you are going to want to cut your losses before they get too dramatic.

And if the open interest is too low, it's going to take a long time to find a buyer. To sell an option, although it seems like magic on the computer screen, you still have to find a real buyer to take an option off your hands. When open interest is only 30, that means there are only 30 contracts out there, and it might take you a long time to find someone to buy it. That can mean lost profits or catastrophic losses.

Check around, and you will find that there are plenty of options that have an open interest above 100, and some have very high levels of open interest.

## Volume

Volume is another measure of an options popularity. Volume tells you the number of times per day the contracts were traded. The closer you get to expiration, the higher the volume is going to be. Volume can be higher or lower than open interest, but popular options such as on the index fund SPY can have a very high level of volume. A high volume isn't the only thing you are going to look for when deciding whether or not to trade an option, of course, but if the trading volume is high, this is an indicator in the options favor. Like open interest, a high trading volume indicates that it will be relatively easy to get in and out of trades quickly.

## Options Exchanges

Options trading takes place on separate exchanges. They are not traded on the stock floors of the New York Stock Exchange or NASDAQ. Most options exchanges are located in Chicago, and there are several options exchanges. For an individual trader, indeed, for many large traders these days, that is all irrelevant. This is all hidden from you by the broker and by a computer interface. All you know is that you are placing an order to buy or sell an option, and the computer reports back on the trade. How it actually gets executed on the other end isn't that important. But you might want to keep it in the back of your mind that a real person is taking the other side of the trade. That can help you to make better trading decisions since you might think about whether a given trade would be something other people are going to be interested in. Usually, however, that isn't too much of a problem. The reason is that the options market is large, and although it is not as large as the stock market, there are enough people around to get the full range of different and competing interests represented. Sometimes when a trade seems like a disaster for you, someone else might feel they can do something with it. What their reasons are you can't possibly know, and it really doesn't matter anyway.

## The Market Maker

Options markets have so-called "market makers". In the old days, these were high flying individuals that made large trades. Today they are likely people with large accounts that work for major institutions like major banks. The purpose of the market maker is to keep the options market running and running as smoothly as possible. Market makers will take the other side of many trades. The point of doing this is largely to keep the market as "liquid" as possible. If you are not sure what liquid means, basically liquid means how easy it is to convert an asset into cash. Something that takes six months to sell is less liquid than something you can sell in 1-2 days. As for options themselves, liquidity means you have the opportunity to purchase and trade options quickly. Sometimes, if you are doing lower volume trades, the market maker might help you by taking the other side of the trade. Once again, we can't always guess the motivations of the market maker or anyone else taking the other side of the trade, and it's not really worth worrying about it. The only thing to think about as an individual options trader is getting in and out of trades when you need to.

In the next chapter, we will discuss the topic pertaining to the so-called "Greeks". Learning about the Greeks will explain how options prices are determined. You will learn specific values and relationships that will tell you how much the price of an option will change in response to a variation in the asset underlying in the contract. You will also learn how much the price of an option will drop in response to "time decay" and some other factors that can influence option pricing.

# Chapter 3: The Greeks

In this chapter, we are going to look at five important parameters that an option has that go by the name "the Greeks". Understanding these parameters will help you estimate where an options price is going to go when different factors that impact that price change. Options pricing is based on mathematical formulas, but you don't need to understand the details. The Greeks will help you make estimations at a glance once you understand what they are all about. Your brokerage trading platform will allow you to look up the Greeks for any option so that you can make the best choices for your investments.

## Delta

The first Greek parameter that we are going to look at is called delta. In many cases, this is the most important of the Greeks. It describes the relationship between the valuation of the stock in question and the options contract. More specifically, it tells us how the price of the option changes in response to variations pertaining to the variation of the equities on the stock market. Consider call options first. The value is given in percentage terms, and if you think of the stock price rising or falling by a dollar, that means the price of the option will rise and fall by the fraction listed as delta. In other words, the option price will change by:

Delta x change in stock price x 100

So, if delta is 0.6, if the underlying price of the equity increased by $1, the price of the contract will rise by 60 cents per share, for a total of $60. If the stock price had only risen by 50 cents instead, then the option price would rise by 30 cents on a per-share basis, or by $30.

These figures show how dramatic options prices can change with small changes in share price. If you are trading options on Apple, Netflix, Tesla, or Google, for example, a one-dollar change in share price is not all that significant. And by extension, a 50-cent change in share price certainly isn't very significant.

Keep in mind, of course, that these cuts both ways. If the valuation of the equity drops by one dollar, the price of the option is going to drop by 60 cents per share if delta is 0.60. One thing this tells you is that you have to keep a close eye on your options trades so that you can get out of bad trades before they become disasters. However, trades can also change direction quickly, since we are talking about relatively small price movements on the stock market. In some of my trades, I had stuck it out when the price of an option dropped by $50 and then saw it rise by $120 in a matter of hours. Panic is not a reason to get out of a trade. We will be discussing this later.

Delta is not a fixed quantity. You will see that it changes depending on changing conditions in the markets. The more in the money an option is, the higher the delta is going to be. Options that are significantly in the money will have delta values that approach 1.0, so their prices can really move with changes in the stock price. If a contract happens to be out of the money, delta will be smaller. A rule of thumb you can use is that for an equity that is at the money, delta is 0.5. Then, for an options deal that is in the money, it will have delta higher than 0.5, while options contracts that are out of the money will have delta lower than 0.5. You can see how this will work to make out of the money options less lucrative. For example, and out of the money option might have a delta of 0.25, so that a $1 increase in the valuation of the equity might only bump the price up $25.

But this also raises the issue of tradeoffs. Options contracts with are out of the money are more affordable to buy, and you can still earn significant profits. Apple is trading at $293 a share as I am writing this, and you can buy a $302 call for $247. Delta is 0.2862. A $1 rise in the stock price is only a 0.34% change, so that is not something outlandish to expect. That would earn you a $29 profit on a $247 investment, a 12% ROI which isn't too shabby. Of course, you can earn more from in the money options, but a

$290 call would require a $793 investment. So how much you can invest is obviously going to be a part of weighing what you trade.

Unfortunately, a lot of online articles, usually written by people who are financially trained but not active options traders, give a lot of bad advice. One thing you are going to see discussed on many websites is advice that you shouldn't trade out of the money options. The truth is that depends on the situation. Later we will discuss situations where trading out of the money options can be a viable strategy.

Now let's turn our attention briefly to put options. The concept is the same, but when you look at put options, you are going to see delta listed as a negative quantity. This is because of the inverse relationship between share price and a put option. Remember that with a contract for a put option, as the share valuation drops, the valuation of the contract increases. Conversely, when share prices rise, the valuation of the corresponding contract decreases. As such, the point of a put options contract is to be able to sell declining shares at a higher price, and the negative delta expresses this fact.

Otherwise, delta for a put option means the same thing. So, you can take a drop in share price and use delta to estimate how the price of the option would change, in the inverse manner described.

As the expiration date approaches, you'll see delta getting very small for out of the money options. Again, that doesn't mean you can't profit from out of the money options.

Remember that delta is dynamic. As the price shifts and time passes, delta might change as well. So, if you look up delta for an option today, it might be different three days from now. You need to keep track of these parameters on a regular basis, so you understand what is going on and what the possibilities are.

In the chart below, we show a perfect example of why these fluctuations are important for options traders. In a short time, frame after the market opened, the stock gained a dollar and twenty-four cents. So, with large, high volume stocks, one dollar or more fluctuations are easily going to happen, and this can cause big swings in options prices (and they might represent opportunities for profits). Notice that the stock also dropped back down but rose back up over $205 per share by the closing bell.

# Theta

Next, we consider a parameter called theta. The purpose of this Greek is to tell you how much value the option is going to lose due to time decay. The losses that you will see from this occur every single day at the market open. So, once the decay happens at the market open, then theta won't impact the option again until the following day. The decline in options price due to theta can be significant, but it can also be overwhelmed by other factors impacting price. We just saw that delta can lead to large changes in options price, and if you have delta at 0.54, theta at -0.12, and the stock rises by $1 at market open, when all is said and done you actually have a 42-cent gain per share, or $42. Of course, if things are not moving your way with the stock, or the delta on an out of the money option is small, that means that theta is going to be working against you.

Theta is expressed as a negative value because it always means the price of the option is going to decline because of time decay when a new trading day opens. This is true for both call and put options, and so theta is always expressed as a negative number, ranging from 0.0 to -1.0. Realistic values range between -0.13 and -0.30. As time to expiration approaches, theta values tend to increase. Also, out of the money options tend to have smaller theta values. However, out of the money options get *all* of their pricing value from time value or extrinsic value, even though their price will fluctuate because of delta. To take an example, consider a stock trading at $220 per share, and suppose we have an out of the money call option with a strike price of $235. At 39 days to option expiration, the price of this option is $408. Theta is -0.105, and delta is 0.29. The extrinsic value is $408, and the intrinsic value is $0. Under the same conditions with 5 days to expiration, delta has dropped to 0.05, and theta has dropped to -0.082. The option is only priced at $160 at this point.

Let's compare values for an in the money call option. Suppose that we have the same $235 strike price, but with a share price of $240. At 39 days to expiration, the price of the option is $1,295.

Delta is 0.60, theta is -0.129, and the option has $795 in extrinsic value with $500 in intrinsic value. At five days to expiration, the price is $670, delta is 0.71, and theta is -0.317. The extrinsic value of this option is $170, and the intrinsic value is $500 at this point.

This example shows us a few important things. The first is that without the money options, buying and holding them over a significant period is foolish. It is this fact that misleads many people that write about options trading to make a mistake to say you shouldn't trade out of the money options. In the trading strategies chapter for calls and puts, we will discuss this in more detail.

We also notice that the intrinsic value is the difference between the share price and the strike price. So close to expiration, as extrinsic value is declining, and in the money, option can make large profits from changing share prices as delta gets closer to 1.0.

The important thing about theta is to have an awareness of it and to be ready for it to work its wicked ways each morning when you hold the options overnight. As we said earlier, whether or not theta turns out to be important for your specific trades is going to be something that depends on the situation.

# Gamma

Gamma is a bit of a more obscure Greek. For math geeks out there, it's a second derivative term. Or in English, it tells you the rate of change of another parameter. In this case, gamma tells us how delta is going to change, in response to a price change. Gamma is the same value for both calls and puts. It's also usually a small value.

Going back to our example, take call and put options with a strike price of $223, and an underlying share price of $220. Gamma for both the call and the put is 0.04. This means that if the share price goes up a dollar, delta for the call will rise by about 0.04, but delta for the put option will decline by 0.04. So, a rising share price will make delta grow for a call option, but it's going to make delta shrink for a put option. In this example that we are using, before the stock price increases, delta for the call is a bit more than 0.37, while for the put, it's -0.63. After the rise in share price by one dollar, delta for the call rises to 0.42, while for the put, it declines to -0.58.

It can be handy to know gamma depending on how deeply you're getting into the analysis. However, most individual traders don't pay much attention to it. I'd say that especially for a beginner spending time worrying about gamma isn't particularly productive. You should devote your time to delta and theta, which will help you focus on what is important for coming profits or losses.

# Vega

The next Greek is Vega, which is related to the implied volatility of an option. Remember that with options, it is all about probabilities that the option is going to end up in the money. The higher the probability that this is going to happen, the higher the price of the option, and therefore more profits for options traders. Assuming that some readers are new to the world of options, let's explain volatility just briefly so that everyone knows what we are talking about.

You probably have a commonsense notion of volatility, and you can visualize it on any mathematical graph, and certainly on a stock chart. Volatility is a reference to the amount of fluctuation in the price when it comes to stock. If the price is making wild price swings, that is having large changes in price up and down for a given time period, then that's high volatility. Low volatility would be more of a smooth curve. Maybe the price is steadily going upward, but there isn't much fluctuation.

Of course, generally speaking, stock price charts are not smooth. There is an inherent amount of volatility baked into the system. This occurs from the random nature of the business. People are buying and selling shares, and fluctuating supply and demand is causing the price to move around basically in random ways, in addition to the overall price trend. But not all stocks fluctuate in the same manner. Stocks that are in heavy demand often have high amounts of volatility, since heavy demand can mean lots of buying and selling activity.

You can visualize volatility just looking at a stock chart, and it's pretty intuitive to determine which stocks are more volatile and which stocks are less volatile. At the same time, this is also precisely quantified. Each stock has a measure of its volatility, which is called Beta. You can look up beta for any stock using your brokerage provided trading platform or on free sites like Yahoo Finance.

Here is how to understand the values given for beta. The larger beta is, the more volatile the stock is. The way this is measured is that the average volatility for the entire market is calculated and assigned a value of 1.0. This means that any stock that has a beta that is higher than 1.0 is more volatile than the market average. If beta is 1.25, that means the stock is 25% more volatile than the market average. If beta were 1.4, that would mean the stock was 40% more volatile than average. When beta is less than 1.0, that means the stock is more quiescent, or less volatile than the market average. Beta can also be negative. That means that the stock is actually fluctuating against the market. So, when the overall market is increasing in price, that stock is decreasing, and vice versa. As you might imagine, negative beta values are actually pretty rare.

For options, it is implied volatility that we are interested in. This is a measure of what volatility is expected to be in the future. This can have a large impact on options prices. This goes back to that fundamental principle, which is that the higher the probability that the option ends up in the money, the higher the price of the option. More volatility means that probability is going to be higher. In fact, high levels of volatility can really cause options prices to rise. Implied volatility is expressed as a percentage.

Implied volatility tends to get large when there is an expectation of something that is going to impact the price of shares. The quintessential example of this is when there is an upcoming earnings call. Earnings calls are something that is big in the options world. If you are an options seller, you might want to avoid earnings calls. So maybe for that week, you don't trade. But for options buyers, earnings calls represent a big opportunity. The key here is to get in on your trade a couple of weeks prior to the earnings call of a big stock. Stock prices change a lot when there is an earnings call, depending on whether or not the company was profitable and more importantly, whether they managed to beat expectations or not. In the weeks leading up to the earnings call, implied volatility gets larger and larger. For some stocks like Tesla or Netflix, implied volatility can get quite large, over 50%.

One strategy you can use is to buy an option a bit of time out before the earnings call and then sell it the afternoon before the earnings call.

Let's see how implied volatility impacts options pricing. We'll go with a $220 share price again and say that we are 10 days to expiration with a strike price of 223. We'll take a relatively average implied volatility of 18%. A call option is $141, and a put option is $439 under these conditions. To understand the impact of implied volatility, we'll keep everything else constant.

Now move to 5 days to expiration. If implied volatility hadn't changed, the call option would be worth $74, and the put option would be $373. That is due to the effects of time decay. However, if the implied volatility had risen to 35%, the call option would be $232, and the put option would be $531. So, you could sell either option for a profit just from the increase in implied volatility alone. And remember, the call option is out of the money, but despite 5 days of time decay, it has increased in value because of the increase in implied volatility.

Now let's go to 2 days left to expiration and suppose that implied volatility is 55%. Now the call option is $230, and the put option is $529, leaving everything else unchanged. The prices haven't changed much, but there has been a lot of time decay, and the increase in time decay is not impacting the options prices hardly at all because of the high level of implied volatility. In fact, at this point, theta is sitting at -0.85 for both the call and the put option. If implied volatility goes up to 65%, the price of the call goes up to $292 and the put to $592.

In some cases, with highly sought-after stocks, if big results are expected in an earnings call, implied volatility can go higher than 70%.

So, Vega is the parameter that tells us how the price of the option is going to change in response to a 1-point change in the implied volatility. You will find that Vega is the same for both calls and puts with the same strike price and expiration date.

## Rho

Finally, we come to the last major Greek. This Greek goes by the name rho. It measures the sensitivity of options prices to interest rates. Specifically, a long-term "risk-free" interest rate is used. It changes in the interest rates that are important, and of course, in today's environment interest rates are pretty steady and only change by small amounts when they do. The best example that you can use to understand the "risk-free" interest rate is the interest rate on a ten-year U.S. Treasury. When interest rates rise, this can have a small but negative impact on options pricing. When interest rates fall, there will be a small but positive impact on options pricing. This is not really a Greek to concern yourself within today's environment, where significant changes in interest rates are unlikely and infrequent. Also, it requires a pretty large change in interest rates to produce a measurable impact on options prices.

## Minor Greeks

There are even more "Greeks". They are known as the minor Greeks. The vast majority of options traders don't pay much if any attention to the minor Greeks, so we aren't going to discuss them. Most options traders don't even pay attention to all of the major Greeks, focusing only on delta, theta, and Vega. If you understand delta, theta, and Vega, you have all the information you need in order to be a successful options trader.

# Chapter 4: Swing Trading with Options

The most straightforward way to trade options is to make a bet on the direction of the stock market and buy call or put options accordingly. Most beginning options traders are going to have to start with this method because more advanced strategies are closed off to beginning options traders. That isn't all bad, however, because you should get a feel for the options market before attempting more complicated trades.

## What is Swing Trading?

The type of trading that we are going to be discussing in this chapter can loosely be described as swing trading. If you are not familiar with it, swing trading is a simple trading philosophy, where the idea is to trade "swings" in market prices. In a commonsense kind of way, there is nothing special about swing trading because it's a buy-low and sell-high method of trading with stocks. You can also profit from a stock when the price is declining by "shorting" the stock.

So, what distinguishes swing trading from other types of trading and investing? The main distinction that is important is that swing trading is different from day trading. A day trader will enter their stock position and exit the position on the same trading day. Day traders never hold a position overnight.

Swing traders hold a position at least for a day, which means they will hold their position at a minimum overnight. Then they will wait for an anticipated "swing" in the stock price to exit the position. This time frame can be days to weeks, or out to a few months' maximum.

A swing trader also differs from an investor, since at the most, the swing trader is going to be getting out of a position in a few months. Investors are in it for the long haul and often put their money in companies that they strongly believe in. Alternatively, they are looking to build a "nest egg" over a time period of one to three decades or even more.

Swing traders don't particularly care about the companies they buy stock in. They are simply looking to make a short-term profit. So, although swing traders may not be hoping to make an instant profit like a day trader, they are not going to be hoping for profits from the long-term prospects of a company. A swing trader is only interested in changing stock prices. Even the reasons behind the changes in the stock prices may not be important. So, whether it's

Apple or some unknown company, if it is in a big swing in stock prices, the swing trader will be interested.

The chart below shows the concept of swing trading. If you are betting on falling prices, you can earn profit following the red line in the chart. If you are betting on increasing prices, you would follow the upward trending blue line. A bet on falling prices is often referred to as being short, while a bet on rising prices means you are long on the stock. This, of course, is another difference between swing trading and investing; investors don't short stock.

Swing trading can be used in any financial market. In the chart above, we are actually showing a chart from the Forex (currency exchange) market. The principles are the same, so the specific market we are talking about doesn't really matter, which is why it works with options.

# Support and Resistance

An important concept often used by swing traders is spotting support and resistance. Support refers to a local low price of the stock. It's basically a pricing floor that, for the time being, the stock price is not dropping below. To find support, you just draw straight lines on the stock chart. The share price should touch the support level at least twice in order for it to be a valid level of support.

Resistance is a local high price. So, this is a high price level that the stock is not able to break above. Again, expect it to touch the resistance level at least twice, and drop back down, before you consider a given share price for the resistance level.

As the share price moves in between support and resistance, there are opportunities to buy-low at the support level price and then sell-high at the resistance level. And you can do the reverse in the case of shorting stock. You can enter your position at the relatively high resistance level, then exit your position at the support level.

Of course, support and resistance are not going to be valid price levels for all time, and a stock will often "break out" of support or resistance. This happens when the share price starts a declining trend and goes below the support level, or if it breaks out above the resistance level in an uptrend. These can be more opportunities to make a profit. But, when a stock price is stuck between support and resistance levels, we say it is *ranging*.

## Trade with the Trend

The best thing to happen to a swing trader (or a trader of straight call and put options) is for a stock to enter into a unidirectional trend. So, it could be a trend in upward prices, giving you a chance to make large profits before it starts reversing. Alternatively, of course, trends can head downwards, opening up opportunities for those who are shorting the stock.

Trends can exist in many different time frames. It might only last part of a day, or it could last weeks and even months. Learning to spot trends and take advantage of them, with a sense as to when the trends are going to come to an end, is something that comes with experience and education. A new options trader can benefit by studying educational materials related to both swing and day trading so they know what to look for in stock charts to spot not only trends worth getting into, but also how to spot a trend reversal which would eat up your profits.

The chart below of AutoZone stock is a simple example of this concept. It's a dream trade, with prices going steadily up with time. But remember nothing lasts forever.

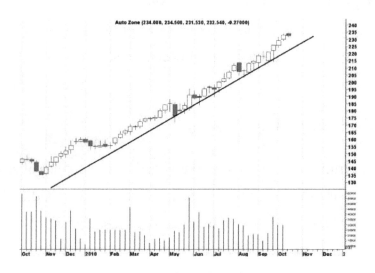

Auto Zone (234.000, 234.500, 231.530, 232.540, -0.27000)

Trading with a trend is definitely something you'll want to look for as an options trader. The time scale of the trend is going to be something important, of course, because you are going to be concerned about time decay when trading options. Time decay is a concept that a swing trader does not have to worry about.

So rather than being beholden to specific rules, like saying you are going to trade options like a day trader or like a swing trader, an options trader has to be flexible. You will need to be ready to take advantage of very short term moves in stock price that only last for a day or less, and you'll also want to be in trades that can last days to weeks or even months.

# Swing Trading Options

Since options are time-limited, they are a natural fit for the concept of swing trading. Although many of the advanced strategies attempt to take out the direction of share price movement from the equation, if you are buying single call or put options in order to make a profit, then you're definitely behaving at least in a qualitative sense like a swing trader.

Since put options gain in value when stock prices are declining, buying put options is like shorting stock. It's actually quite a bit more accessible, however. In order to short stock, you must have a margin account so that you can borrow shares from the broker. The basic idea of shorting stock is to borrow shares from the broker when the stock price is at a relatively high point and sell them. After this, the trader will wait for the share price to drop. Then when the share price is low enough to make a profit, the trader will buy the shares back and return them to the broker.

Of course, shorting stock using options is far easier. The reason is you never have to buy the stock to make a profit from the declining price. You simply profit from prices of put options which will increase as the stock price goes down.

# Going Long on a Stock

If you believe that the price of a stock is going to rise, then you want to buy call options. So, call options represent the most straightforward or common-sense way to trade options. When you buy a call option, you are betting on that stock. Another way to say this is that you are bullish on the stock.

A good way to go about trading options is to pick a few companies and limit yourself to trading them. The reason is that you are going to have to be paying attention to the markets, company news, and general financial news for any option that you invest in. If you spread yourself too thin, you are not going to be able to stay on top of things and will find yourself getting caught up in losing trades. The best approach is to keep your trading limited in scope so that you can know what is going on. That doesn't mean you only trade a single call option; you might trade a large number of them on the same stock.

There are two ways to go about swing trading options. The first way is to look for ranging stocks that are trapped in between support and resistance. Then you can trade call and put options that move with the swings. So, the idea of this type of trading is very simple. First, you need to study a stock of interest and determine what the price levels of support and resistance are. Then, when the price drops to the support level, you buy call options. Now hold them until the price goes back up near resistance. It can be a good idea to exit your trades before the price gets all the way to resistance so that you don't end up losing some of your potential profits if the price reverses before you get rid of the options.

Trend trading call options can also be very lucrative. In this case, you are looking for significant news and developments related to the stock or even the economy at large. For example, when a company announces that it had big profits, this can be an opportunity to earn money with call options, as the price will go up by large amounts as people start snapping up the stock. When trading in this fashion, you're going to need to know how to spot trend reversals. We will talk about that later in this chapter. The idea is basically the same when you identify a trend in the making, you buy call options, and then ride the trend until you are satisfied with the level of profit and sell the options.

Again, it can't be emphasized too much. You always need to take time to decay into account when trading options. So, remember that with each passing day, your options are going to automatically lose value. Check theta to find out how much value they are going to lose. And as we discussed before, often, other factors overwhelm time decay in the short term.

A big opportunity with call options is trading on index funds. SPY, which we mentioned earlier, is one of the top choices for trading call options. In the case of SPY, you are going to be paying attention to overall economic news to look for opportunities. Any information related to the economy at large can cause large moves with this index fund. This includes changes in interest rates (or even leaving them the same when that is what the market would prefer), announcements of GDP growth rates, changes in trade policy, or release of jobs numbers. One of the best things about options on SPY is that they are extremely liquid, making it very easy to get in and out of your trades. You can also trade many other index funds, tracking virtually anything financial.

## Shorting Stock Using Put options

Put options may be one of the most powerful tools available to the individual trader. To earn profits from shorting stock, you have to be a big player in the market. That means you have to get a margin account and have enough financial resources that you are able to borrow large numbers of shares from the broker. Most new traders are not going to be at that point. Keep in mind that to earn profits from shorting stock, you'll have to be shorting 100 shares or more of stock in order to make money.

With put options, you can leverage the stock through the option. By investing in Put options, you get control of the stock and earn profits from the price movements in the stock without actually having to buy shares. A single put option might cost $30, $100, or $400, but you will control 100 shares.

Some traders actually hope to profit by selling the shares when they buy put options, but most traders simply want to get into a put option early when a downward trend in stock price is expected, and then sell the put option for a profit when stock prices have actually declined. The same basic things to look for apply, except you'll be doing it in reverse. So, you can trade put options for profits when stocks are ranging. In this case, you start the trade by purchasing put options when stock prices are relatively high, at the resistance level. Then you hold your put options until prices drop down again to support and sell them for a profit.

Likewise, for an options trader, downward trends in stock prices are just as nice as upward trends. When a downward trend is developing, you invest in Put options and then sell them when the stock price has dropped enough such that you are taking an acceptable profit. As with call options, traders using put options will need to learn about signals that indicate trend reversals so that you have some quantitative tools to help you make solid trades.

Keep in mind there are no guarantees on the options market. When trading options, we are really looking for probabilities. This means that you can expect to have some losing trades, and the goal is to be profitable overall without worrying about specific trades.

## Tools to Spot Trend Reversals

Swing traders use tools that help them estimate changes in the direction of stock market prices. Some of these tools are more qualitative in nature and involve spotting particular chart patterns that usually indicate a trend reversal is coming. You can think of these tools more in the sense of being rules of thumb or even "art of trading".

Many other tools used by swing traders are more mathematically based. These tools go under the umbrella of *technical analysis*. We aren't going to have space in this book to delve into all the details and tools used, but we will cover the most fundamental tools which are enough to get you started, and in fact, are often all that you need. Let's get started looking at a few chart patterns.

## Chart Patterns That Indicate Trend Reversals

A trend reversal is important for an options trader because it's a point that you will use to either enter a trade or exit a trade. Over the decades, traders have come to recognize certain chart patterns that will indicate a coming trend reversal. This is a bet, in a sense. The given chart pattern is no guarantee a reversal is coming, but most of the time that will be the case. Chart images below were created by Altaf Qadir on Wikipedia.

The first chart patter we are going to look at is the "head and shoulders". This pattern occurs at the top of an upward trend before the price begins declining. It is characterized by three peaks in the chart. The middle peak will be the highest, and it will be flanked by two smaller peaks that are generally the same height. The pattern emerges because there are still traders coming into the stock, but the numbers are such that not enough of them are still entering the position in order to push prices up further. So, as they enter their positions, these late arrivals push up prices a little bit, and then it drops back down again. When the pattern is forming, prices drop down to a level called the neckline. Then they rise back up.

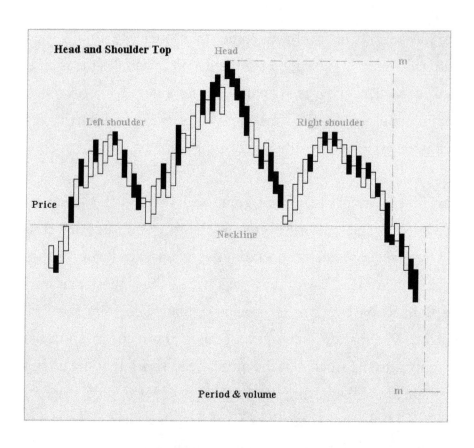

Head and Shoulder Top

Head

Left shoulder

Right shoulder

m

Price

Neckline

Period & volume

m

By the point of the right shoulder, traders are going to be looking to take profits. So, they will be exiting their positions, and as the number of people selling increases, the increased supply of the stock on the market relative to willing buyers will start pushing prices down. So, if you are trading call options and the stock underlying the call shows this pattern, it is a good time to sell.

You can simply flip the chart over to see a trend reversal developing after declining stock prices.

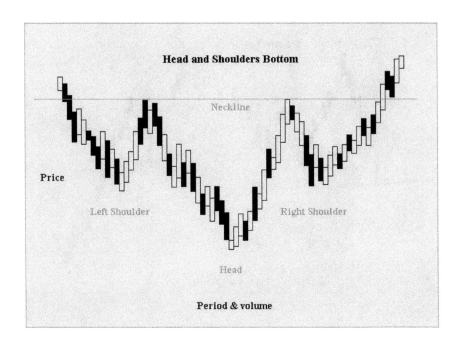

A double top is the same type of phenomenon, but with only two price peaks.

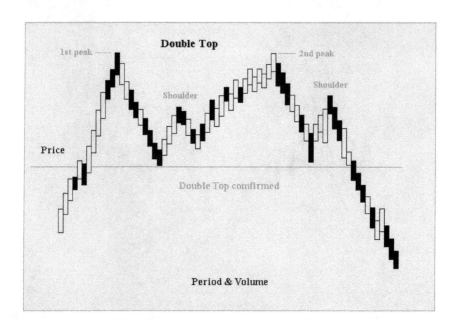

Next, we consider a cup and handle. This takes place in an uptrending stock before there is a large breakout. In this case, the stock will rise to a peak, and then gradually drop down in a relatively smooth fashion, forming a bowl shape. So, it will drop to a minimum and then gradually start rising to the previous level, which forms the "cup" part of the pattern. Then there will be a period where the stock price is ranging between two values, not really doing much. This is the handle part of the pattern. After the handle, the stock is likely to break out to the upside.

There are many chart patterns like these used by traders, but we can only cover a few because there are large numbers of them, and it would be outside the scope of this book. There are many online resources available that can be used in order to study and learn chart patterns. Consider using the site Investopedia to learn all of them if you are so inclined.

# Candlestick Charts

Candlestick charts show stock prices divided up into small trading periods. This is done so that you can determine changing investor behavior before there is a major trend reversal. Each trading period is a microcosm of the trading day, week, or month, with its own opening and closing price, and high and low price. This way, you can see whether or not investors are in a buying or selling mood, and how strong that mood actually is.

Candlesticks are colored according to whether or not the closing price for the trading period was above or below the opening price. If the closing price is higher than the opening price, that is a bullish candlestick, and these are normally green in color (although different trading platforms sometimes use different coloring schemes). Candlesticks have "wicks" that are sometimes called shadows that extend out of the top and bottom, indicating the high and low for the stock for that trading period. A candlestick chart is illustrated below.

By examining how candlesticks are forming in a series, it can be possible to spot trend reversals in price. Candlesticks can be used on many different time frames, from 1 minute to 5 minutes, to 1 hour, 4 hours and more. The time scale to use is going to depend on what your goals are at the moment. If the price of a stock is fast-moving and you are looking to sell options to make a profit by exiting your positions, you might want to go with a 5-minute time frame, for example.

There are many different patterns on candlestick charts that can indicate future direction in price. Remember that price is really a reflection of demand for a given security, so declining price means that fewer buyers are willing to close a sale for the given price, and the price must continually drop until an equilibrium between buyers and sellers is reached. As an options trader, you are looking for changes or reversals in the trend.

When you see three candlesticks in a row of the same type, this can be an indication of a trend reversal. We actually see this in two spots in the chart above. These have been marked to draw your attention to them in a reproduction of this chart here, showing a trend reversal turning into a significant downward trend in price:

This pattern goes by the name "three black crows" when there are three bearish (or red) candlesticks in a row. Although the sighting of a black crow may be taken by some to be an indication of bad luck, the term "black crow" in this context is really historical. Options trading began in the 1920s but was suspended in the Great Depression and not revived again until 1973. Prior to the widespread adaptation of colored printing, candlestick charts used solid black candlesticks to represent bearish trading sessions, thus the name "black crows". For stock traders, declining prices are always a bad sign, so that is another reason why "bearish" denotes a bad situation, but remember that as an options trader, you can profit in either case. If you saw a chart like the one above, the three red candlesticks in a row would be a very good indication that you should buy put options. Then, you hold your put options until either a) you have made a level of profit that you find acceptable, or b) you see signs in the charts of another trend reversal, which is going to start eating into possible profits and possibly even turn them into losses.

When you see three green or bullish candlesticks in a row, this is a sign of a coming uptrend, and in the business, it is known as "three white soldiers". Again, the name is historical. It comes from the fact that in the days before color printing and computer screens, bullish candlesticks were outlined and hence "white" in color.

Another important candlestick patterns every options trader should be aware of is the engulfing pattern. This can happen at the end of a downtrend in prices or at the end of an upward trend in prices. In either case, and engulfing pattern occurs when a candle of the dominant trend type is followed by a large candle of the opposite type, such that the following candle completely covers the length of the previous candle. This concept is illustrated below.

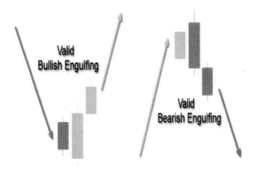

Let's focus on the bullish engulfing pattern to understand what is going on here. Notice that the closing price, which is indicated by the bearish candlestick to the left, is a bit higher than the opening price of the bullish candlestick immediately to its left. This indicates that at the start of the trading period, people were still selling off, pushing prices down lower. In fact, in the example given, you can see a wick sticking out the bottom indicating that prices continued to drop. However, by the end of the trading period, prices reversed and went much higher than the previous close, and also higher than the previous open. This indicates that the trend is reversing because buyers are now pushing prices up with increasing demand. In the given example, there is a follow up bullish candlestick, but that isn't strictly necessary although the appearance of one would increase confidence. It is the trend that starts to develop over the next few candlesticks that are important. In the example given, we see that at the next time period prices continue to be pushed higher. This kind of pattern would indicate that it's either a good time to buy call options on the underlying stock or a good time to sell put options if you've got some in your inventory.

In the bearish example, it's a similar situation but with everything reversed. In the engulfing candle, remember that the top of a red or bearish candle is the opening price for the trading session, while the bottom of the candle is the closing price. So, in this case, the trading session for the engulfing candle opened with a small continuation of the previous trend – and prices jumped higher. Then they were pushed down by a large amount, even further down than the opening price (and indeed for the low price) of the previous trading session. This indicates that the opening price of the bearish candle indicated only a slight increase in prices; in other words, demand was starting to peter out. The fact that the candle engulfs the previous one indicates that the selloff became overwhelming, as compared to the previous trading session.

Another important candlestick pattern that is often used is a "hammer". Depending on the orientation of the hammer, it can be a plain hammer or an inverted hammer. It is also called a shooting star if present at the start of an uptrend. A hammer has a wick that only comes out of one end of the candlestick and a relatively narrow body. This means first of all that opening and closing prices (regardless of whether we are talking about a bullish or bearish situation) were fairly close to each other. Second, it means that during the trading session, prices were pushed strongly in one direction, only to be pushed way back towards the opening price level for the trading session. A shooting star occurs when an inverted hammer occurs at the top of an uptrend, indicating that prices were pushed up high, only to drop down below the opening price (so for a shooting star you are looking for a bearish candlestick.

Here are two examples so that you understand what a hammer or inverted hammer actually looks like:

**Inverted Hammer**      **Shooting Star**

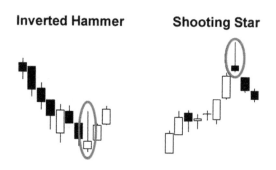

To get a hammer, you just flip it over.

While these are the main trend reversal signals with candlesticks, there are literally dozens of them. You can learn what they are and how to spot them using many resources, including free resources that are available online. A good options trader, however, is not going to rely on only using one or two techniques, so you don't need to devote your entire life to studying candlestick charts. Looking to spot the most compelling chart reversal signals is usually enough for most traders when used in conjunction with other tools.

Be calm when looking at stock charts. You don't need to enter or exit a trade in a matter of seconds when trading options in most situations. So, it isn't necessary to spend hours memorizing candlestick.

## Moving Averages

One of the most powerful tools that you can use in order to spot trend reversals is using moving averages. Moving averages are used in conjunction with candlestick charts by most stock traders, but in my opinion moving averages are actually a stronger signal indicating a trend reversal, and it is even possible to rely only on moving averages in a lot of cases. But to play it safer, a typical approach would be to look at moving averages for a trend reversal and then confirm by looking at the candlestick patterns.

First, let's take a step back and make sure we understand what a moving average is. Anyone understands the concept of an average, we take a set of data points and add them up, and then divide by the number of data points. A moving average is like this, except at each point along the line, we compute the average at that point. So, the average at each point is going to be different and reflect market conditions at the point in question. Moving averages require that you specify the number of points used in the calculation. Note that stock charts extend far back in the past, so you could use 10 points, 30 points, 200 points or more.

For stocks, we can compute averages on nearly any time frame we desire. For the sake of simplicity, suppose that we are averaging daily, using the closing price. So, each point on our chart, assuming that we are using a candlestick chart is going to be one day. To compute the moving average for 9 days, we could create a 9-day moving average curve and add it to our chart. At each day along the chart, it would get the past 9 days of data and compute the average. So, you can see why it's "moving", as it goes to the next day on the chart, the first day used in the previous calculation drops off and is replaced with the current day.

If the stock prices used to calculate the average are just added up and then divided by the number of days in the calculation, then we call this a simple moving average. Many traders get by quite well using simple moving averages, and there really isn't an argument that you can frame against them. We are not looking for ultimate precision. We are looking for indicators that trader sentiment on a given stock is changing.

However, many traders argue against the use of simple moving averages. The reason that you might not want to use them is that notice the simple moving average treats all prices with equal relevance. That might be fine if you are only using a moving average over the course of a few days, but the longer the time frame you use in your moving average, the less relevant prices in the past are to the calculation. The simple moving average fails to recognize this basic fact.

To get around this, different types of moving averages were created to weight the data, so that more recent prices would get more "weight" in the calculations. The most popular type of moving average used for weighting is called an exponential moving average. Another popular method used is called a Hull moving average, after its creator. These types of moving averages are pretty accurate, and you will notice that they track the actual pricing trends quite closely.

One of the benefits of moving average curves is that they remove noise from a stock chart. Rather than seeing the typical jagged up and down zig-zag line that you are used to seeing, you will see a smooth curve that represents the real, underlying trend in stock prices.

To use moving averages to spot trend reversals, we will add two moving average curves to the stock chart. These moving averages will have different periods, or in plain English, they will use a different number of trading sessions. So, if you are using a chart of daily stock prices, the moving averages will use a different number of days for each curve. The point of doing this is to see whether or not the short-term price movements are going higher or lower than the long-term average at each point. When this type of event happens, this usually indicates a trend reversal. That apparent trend reversal can be compared to other indicators like candlestick patterns to confirm what you are seeing with the moving average curves. In most situations, you can be pretty confident that a crossover of moving average curves will mean a coming trend reversal.

Different choices are used to spot trend reversals with moving average curves. For example, a popular method is to use 50-day and 200-day moving averages. These curves work pretty well under a wide variety of circumstances, but I find the 200-day moving average too long. Let me tell you why.

When you are looking for a long-term moving average, you have to keep in mind that it's going to be impacted by many factors. For example, it might be impacted by earnings calls, and the more you extend the moving average into the past, the more impact moving averages are going to have. Earnings calls can have a pretty dramatic impact on stock prices. Over the past year, there have been earnings calls that have moved stock prices by $20, $40, and more in a single day or even in overnight after-hours trading. The impact of earnings calls can be long-lasting. For example, a boost in share prices from an earnings call might set a new support pricing floor for the stock in question. But it may not be long-lasting, and so it's an outlier data point that is distorting prices.

Also, no matter what, when it comes to tomorrow's stock price, recent events and stock prices are simply a lot more relevant. And trading options, unless you are investing in LEAPs, you're definitely interested in short-term price movements, often of 30 days or less. In fact, many options traders only trade on weekly time scales. So, what the stock was doing 200 days ago doesn't seem as relevant to what it's going to be doing in the next few days.

For this reason, I like to use a 9-day moving average in conjunction with a 20-day moving average, or you can use a 50-

day moving average. My advice is to try different values and see how it works for you. Apply these moving averages to *past* stock market data, so that you can get a feel for how it really worked with real data. Your trading time frame will also be important. Shorter time frames that you are looking at to enter or exit trades are going to demand shorter moving averages.

So, what are we looking for? We are looking for the behavior of the short-term moving average curve with respect to the long-term moving average curve. Sticking to my preferred values, we are looking for the 9-day moving average curve to either move below or above the 20-day moving average curve. When the short-term moving average moves below the long-term moving average – this is a very strong signal that stock prices are going to decline in short order. On the other hand, when the short-term moving average goes above the long-term moving average, we have the reverse condition – so this is a strong indication that there is a coming uptrend in stock prices. Always confirm by looking at other signals, such as the candlestick chart, before entering or exiting a position.

When we see the short-term moving average drop below the long-term moving average, this is called a "death cross". Once again, the terminology used is reflective of the mentality of straightforward stock traders, where they view increasing stock prices as strictly positive, and declining stock prices as strictly negative. As an options trader, you should adopt a view that a particular move in one direction or the other is neutral. So, when you see a "death cross", you should consider investing in Put options. If you are already invested in call options, a death cross is a selling signal. Here is an example, via Market Watch, of a death cross for Apple stock prices:

Here, the green line represents the short-term moving average, while the red line represents the long-term moving average. Of course, prices are going to fluctuate up and down constantly, but by looking at the relationship between the two curves, you can not only spot buy and sell points but also false signals. For example, a bit after the death cross in the figure, we notice that the stock price started climbing, which may have led novice traders to buy

88

calls or to sell put options. But if you are looking at the moving average curves, you'll see that the short-term moving average remained below the long-term moving average even as the stock prices momentarily rose to a higher level. Whenever you see the short-term moving average staying clearly below the long-term moving average, you should take the view that bearish conditions are still in existence no matter what the stock price is doing in the moment. Since the stock market is a pretty chaotic system, we can expect that it is going to be doing a lot of up and down movement that is not going to be significant at all over any time period of interest. And you can see clearly from the figure that the indication given to us by the death cross proved quite accurate, as the curve of stock prices continued to decline to a significantly lower value.

When the short-term moving average goes above the long-term average, this is called a golden cross, because it is an indicator of a coming upward trend in stock prices. A golden cross is, therefore, an indicator that represents a buy signal for call options and a sell signal for put options. The example below shows simple moving averages, using a 50-day simple moving average for the short-term curve, and a 200-day moving average for the long-term curve. This particular example is a textbook example, showing a very strong upward trend that followed the golden cross:

Pay attention to the slopes of the moving average curves. When one of the curves has a much stronger slope than the other curve, this can indicate that the trend is either going to be weak or strong. In the example above, the short-term moving average curve has a larger slope, and so it grows faster (for a time), indicating that this is a very strong upward trend in price. You can also note that at the marked entry point in the figure, the candlesticks certainly agree with the information that you are getting from the golden cross. There is a "three white soldiers" pattern just before the golden cross; in fact, there are more than three bullish candlesticks at that point. That is a strong confirmation signal that would give you confidence in using this moving average crossover as an indicator that you should go ahead and invest in call options.

# Relative Strength Indicator

The next item we are going to look at, which can be used in swing trading, is called the relative strength indicator. This is a technical tool that can be used in order to estimate "overbought" and "oversold" conditions. In my opinion, it should not be used as a primary tool, but only to give confidence to the type of information that you are getting from your other tools. So, the general procedure you should utilize is to first look for moving average crossovers. Then confirm with the candlestick chart and then look at the relative strength indicator to solidify the information that you are getting.

The relative strength indicator will put a curve below your stock chart, and it will range over the values 0-100. If the relative strength index is between 30-70, it is considered neutral. If it is above 70, this represents "overbought" conditions. This means that buyers have been too enthusiastic about entering this stock and have pushed the price of the stock up to levels that aren't justified by external conditions. When a stock is overbought, this can be an indication that the price is going to start declining, since the only way out of an overbought stock is to sell it.

However, this technical indicator can only be described as suggestive. In many cases, I have seen stocks labeled as overbought, but the price kept going up and up. At least for a time. For this reason, my advice with the relative strength indicator is to only look at it when you are unsure even after looking at the candlestick charts and the moving averages. For example, you can come to a tentative conclusion with a crossover on the moving averages that the candlestick charts seem to confirm, and if you are still not confident, you can use the relative strength indicator to back up what you think your move should be.

When there are overbought conditions, this indicates that you should sell call options, or alternatively, buy put options. An overbought indicator is a bearish indicator. But again, it's no guarantee by any means.

Overbought conditions will form at the top of an upward trend in prices that are coming to an end.

When the relative strength indicator is 30 or below, this indicates oversold conditions. That means that people have been too active getting out of the stock, and prices are likely to start rising again soon. So oversold conditions are a strong indicator that you should be looking to exit your position if you have been investing input options. If you are looking for stock prices to rise, this could suggest an entry point for buying calls.

Oversold conditions are going to occur at the bottom of a downward trend.

Again, you are probably going to want to be using the relative strength index on a secondary basis. So if you see a golden cross and it seems to be confirmed by the candlestick patterns (which would indicate a trend reversal to the upside), if you can confirm this with an RSI below 30, that is a strong indication that you should be investing in call options or getting out of positions that are invested in Put options.

## Bollinger Bands

Another very popular tool used in swing trading goes by the name of Bollinger bands after its creator. Bollinger bands involves defining some boundaries for a stock, using moving averages. It relies on simple moving averages by default, but you can customize it. It forms "bands" by using a simple moving average and then also plotting one standard deviation above the simple moving average, and one standard deviation below the moving average. The basic idea here is that under normal conditions, a stock is going to stay within a standard deviation of the mean. If it goes outside of this range, then that is an indication that there is going to be a trend reversal. Of course, there are special situations (again, think earnings calls) when this might not be true because breaking news can cause unusually large movements in stock price. However, under normal circumstances, the stock can be reasonably assured to stay within a standard deviation of the mean. After all, that is the meaning of standard deviation.

Bollinger bands are overlaid on the stock chart. Most traders are going to use Bollinger bands in conjunction with candlestick charts, and so you are looking for the candlesticks to fall above or below the Bollinger bands. So, if there has been an upward trend of the stock price and then the price touches or goes outside the upper Bollinger band, that is a point where you can expect a trend reversal in the price to the downside. This means that you would either be investing in puts or selling your positions that were invested in call options.

Alternatively, if prices have been dropping and then the candlesticks touch or go outside the lower Bollinger band, then we can expect a trend reversal to the upside. This is taken to be a signal that you should buy call positions or exit put options.

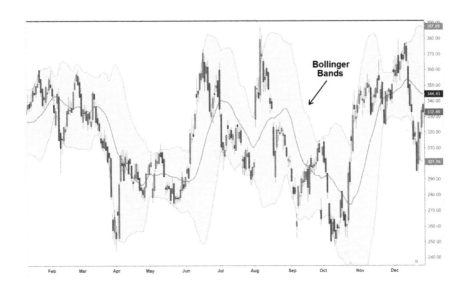

In short, Bollinger bands are a way to dynamically add support and resistance to your stock charts. So, we can take the lower Bollinger band to be supported, while the upper Bollinger band is taken to be supported.

# Chapter 5: The Iron Condor and Iron Butterfly

In the previous chapter, we learned about straight trading of calls or puts. In short, this represents a style of trading that is something that goes along with swing trading stocks. You either want to short the stock, that is bet the price is going to be entering a decline or go long with call options and make profits from rising prices. This is a basic strategy that involves basically making a bet on which direction the stock price is going to move. The cold reality is that while there are certain circumstances when you can make bets on trends in stock prices, that is a very difficult game to play overall. Most professional options traders do not do straight trading of calls and puts, because it is a high-risk bet on stock direction. Instead, they use one or more of several advanced trading strategies.

Advanced trading strategies seek to do one or both of two things. The first thing that advanced trading strategies seek to do is to reduce your risk. This can be done by reducing the probability of engaging in a losing trade or by capping losses. And actually, there are more ways to reduce risk. For example, you can remove the direction of the stock market from the equation, which is something that we are going to talk about here.

## Removing Direction from the Trade

The iron condor is a trading strategy that does something that is quite unusual. Rather than betting on the stock moving one way or the other, it bets instead that the stock is going to stay within a certain range of prices. Over short time periods, unless there is a dramatic event, be it something unpredictable or something expected like an earnings call, stocks are basically going to flail around within a certain narrow confine of pricing. In other words, most stocks will spend most of their time range.

This is where an iron condor comes in. An iron condor is a limited risk strategy that bets that the stock price is going to be trapped within two values over the lifetime of the trade. Now, of course, if you were to trade stocks over a matter of weeks or years, stock prices would probably be hard to pin down within a range. But most traders enter into iron condor positions with time frames of a maximum of 45 days all the way down to a single week.

An iron condor has four "legs". As a new options trader, it is important to become familiar with the jargon, and my legs, all this means is that there are four options involved in the trade. We will spell it out later in the chapter.

# Central Goal of the Iron Condor

The central goal of an iron condor (or an iron butterfly) is that the stock price is going to stay within a bounded range of values over the lifetime of the options contracts. What the stock price does within that time frame really isn't of concern. It might go up, go down, or hardly move at all. For the trader, that isn't important.

All that matters to the trader of the iron condor or iron butterfly is that the stock doesn't move very much. Very much is a relative term for the iron condor, you can define any range you like. The narrower the range, the more money you are going to make. However, that means higher risk. If the stock's price goes outside of the range, this could end up being a losing trade, in the event that the options go to expiration. If you have a smaller range of values, that means that there is a higher probability that the stock is going to go outside the range. You can have a wider range to reduce risk, but that will decrease potential profits as well.

# Iron Condors are Income Strategies

When you buy a call or a put, note that you are buying to open your position. This is a speculation strategy; you are speculating that you can earn profits from certain moves in the stock price.

However, with an iron condor, we meet a new and different way to think about the stock markets and options trading. An iron condor is an income strategy.

This means that you are going to open a position in an iron condor by selling it for a credit. Since an iron condor has four legs, that means it's a trade that involves buying and selling four options simultaneously. But you will be buying options on net as we will see. But the point is not to speculate, although there is always a small amount of speculation in any stock or options trade. The point is to earn income. Many options traders sell iron condors on a revolving basis so that they can receive options premium on a regular basis. Options premium refers to the payments that are put in by people buying options.

As an income strategy, this means that you are going to be selling iron condors, rather than buying them. The idea is that you sell them for a credit, provided the stock price does not violate some conditions that you set on the trade; you get to pocket the credit as a profit.

## The Lower Legs

The lower legs of an iron condor consist of two put options that form the lower boundary or support region for our trade. The boundary is formed using the strike prices of the options. So, we are hoping that the stock price never goes as low as the strike prices of our put options. There are two put options that form the lower boundary of the iron condor. We need the stock prices to be above the strike price of the higher put option at closing to make a profit.

We set this up using what is called a vertical spread. This just means that we have to options of the same type, that have different strike prices on the same stock and with the same expiration date. In this case, you are going to sell the put option that has a higher strike price. The idea with an iron condor is that you are going to be selling options that are out of the money.

Selling a put option can be lucrative, but it carries some risk. The risk is that we would be assigned, meaning that if the share price moved below the strike price of the option minus the breakeven price, a buyer out there might decide to exercise the option. In that case, we would be assigned, and we'd have to buy the shares from the buyer at the strike price on the options contract. Depending on circumstances, this could result in a substantial loss.

However, we can mitigate that loss substantially by simultaneously buying another put option. In this case, we buy another put option with a lower strike price. It's going to be cheaper, and if prices crash, while we will make profits, we will also reduce our risk since we can exercise that option in the event things don't work our way with the overall trade.

To understand how this works, let's make up a simple example. Suppose that a stock is trading at $200 a share, and there are 10 days to expiration. We could sell the $217 put option for $9.37 a share, for a total credit of $937. In the event that the share price moved low enough to make the $217 call profitable for a buyer, we might be assigned, which would mean that we'd have to come up with $217 x 100 = $21,700 in order to buy the shares of stock. That might be an unpleasant thought if the stock price was dropping substantially. For the sake of example, suppose the stock crashed to $200 a share.

However, we can cut our risk by purchasing another put option with a lower strike price. In fact, we could purchase the $210 put for $6.37. Since we are buying this while selling the other option, this means our total profit is cut substantially. In this case, our total profit would be $9.37 - $6.37 = $3. While that is a big cut in possible profits, we've also cut our risks massively. Suppose that the stock price drops below $210, also covering the breakeven price. If the option were exercised, we'd have to buy the 100 shares at $217 a share, resulting in a loss of $21,700. However, since we entered into the contract with the $210 put, we can turn around and sell the shares to someone else. Using the second options contract, we can sell the shares for $210 and make $2,100 back. Now we've reduced our loss to $21,700 - $21,000 = $700.

That may not sound good, but had we not bought the second option, we'd be stuck buying the shares at the sale price. At best, we could sell them on the open market. If they were trading at $200 a share, that means selling them for $20,000. So now our loss is $1,700. So, we've cut our losses by 41%.

## The Other Legs

The upper legs of the trade are created by selling a call option and buying a call option with a higher strike price. The strike price of the lower call option forms the boundary of range for the stock to the upside. So if a stock is trading at $200, and we create an iron condor by selling a put option with a strike price of $195 and buying a put option with a strike price of $190, and then we sell a call option with a strike price of $205 and buy a call option with a strike price of $210, if the stock price stays in between $195-205, we earn profit. On the other hand, we lose if it goes above or below this range. So, with the legs involving the call options, you buy a call option with a certain strike price, and then sell one with a higher strike price.

The basic ideas are the same as compared to what we've looked at before, but in this case, we don't want the price to move very substantially. We are going to be in trouble if it breaks to the upside or the downside.

## The Complete Iron Condor as a Single Trade

When you enter into an iron condor position, you are going to enter it as a single trade. So, you buy a call and a put, and you sell a call and a put, simultaneously. The important point here is that you are selling the position. You have to know that your inner strike prices set the acceptable range over which the price of the stock can move.

The following chart illustrates the iron condor:

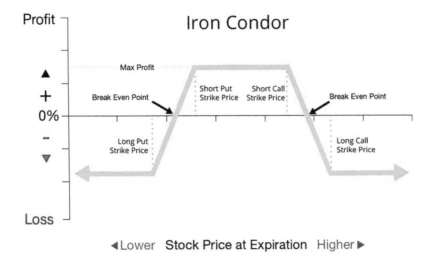

The Iron Condor Relies on Time Decay
=====================================

# The Iron Condor Relies on Time Decay

You can buy an iron condor with respect to any expiration date of options. However, the main strength of the iron condor is time decay. Put another way. You are going to earn more from an iron condor that expires further out in the future. However, most iron condor traders will work in a time frame that ranges between 30-45 days. Some traders will opt for shorter time frames. Many will take a mere week's time frame or 7-14 days. By reducing the amount of time until expiration, you also reduce the probability that the stock is going to move outside the bounded range. So, while buyers are hoping the stock is going to break one way or the other and get outside the range set up by the iron condor, you're playing the role of the house and making the opposite bet.

So, keep the following in mind:

- Less time left, lower risk to seller, but less possible income. In this case, with a shorter time frame on the contract, the probability of the stock exceeding the range set up by the strike prices is lower.

- More time left, higher risk to seller. This is because the stock has more chances to go above or below the range set by the iron condor. However, there is more possible income. With more time left until expiration, you will earn more money from time decay.

Since you are selling a call option with a lower strike price(relative to the call options that you buy) and selling a put option with a higher strike price(relative to a put option that you buy), you are going to get a net credit for the transaction.

## The Iron Butterfly

The iron butterfly is essentially a derivative of the iron condor strategy. So, like the iron condor, the iron butterfly has four options, two puts, and two calls. It will have a put option with a relatively high strike price that you sell. It will have a put option with a relatively low strike price that you buy. Then it will have a call option with a relatively low strike price that you sell, and a call option with a relatively higher strike price that you sell. All options have the same expiration date.

In the case of the iron butterfly, however, you are going to have a call option and a put option that have the same strike prices. This means that for an iron butterfly to be profitable, the share price has to stay on the strike price, which defines the mid-value for the trade. You can see this in the graph for the iron butterfly shown below. It has a spike, rather than a range of prices over which the trade is profitable:

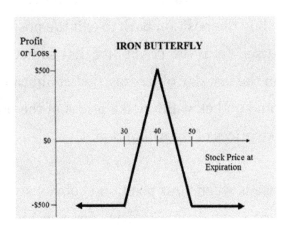

## The Buyback Strategy

Now we are going to briefly mention an important advantage when selling options that can be used to mitigate risk. This is the buyback strategy. In short, if at any time it looks like an option or strategy that you have sold is not working out, or is likely to finish such that you would lose on the trade and have substantial financial obligations, you can buy the trade back. This doesn't mean you buy the trade back from the exact same person (who might not even have it anyway), you can buy it back from any trader on the market. Traders will buy positions back under two circumstances.

The first is that you have simply made a good profit, and the stock is still ranging within the values set by your inner strikes. In this case, you may buy the position back to exit the position, in order to protect yourself from the possibility that something unusual will happen on the last day of trading that could cause the stock to break out, and go below the strike prices of the put option or above the strike prices of the call option.

The second case is when your position is obviously not going to work. In this case, you could buy back your position in order to cap your losses. There is no requirement, as a seller, for you to hold onto the position if it is a losing position. The way that you get out of it is you tell your broker that you want to buy it back. This is done automatically by placing an order to buy that position.

# Maximum Losses

Maximum losses are set to the upside and the downside. If the stock breaks toward the upside, the maximum loss is the difference in the strike prices of the call options plus the breakeven. On the other side, if the stock price collapses so that it ends up lower than the lower strike price of the put options, then the maximum loss is the difference between the strike prices less the breakeven price. The strategy does not require symmetry, but in most cases, traders construct symmetric iron condors or iron butterflies.

# Summary

When do you get into an iron condor or iron butterfly? You do this when you don't expect the share price to move very much. In the case of an iron butterfly, you expect the stock to stay within a range of prices until the expiration date. For the iron butterfly, you expect the share price to stay at the strike price used for the inner call and put options in the trade.

# Chapter 6: Strangles and Straddles

What if there was a strategy you could use to profit if the stock rose high, but you also earned profit if the stock crashed? It sounds too good to be true, but the reality is with options you can do this. The strategies used to accomplish this are called strangles and straddles. In this chapter, we will learn how to set them up, how they work, and when to use them.

## Strangle Options Strategy

The strangle options strategy is designed in a way that is somewhat opposite that of an iron condor. While an iron condor is set up to earn profits if the stock price stays within a certain range, a strangle will earn profit only if the stock price breaks out of this range. It doesn't matter if the price rises or falls; a strangle makes a profit either way. So, this is an ideal strategy to use when you expect big price movements on the stock, but you are not sure which direction the price will go.

The classic situation where a strangle can be used is with an earnings call. Prior to an earnings call, it is not known for sure how the earnings of the company will be reported. The benchmark used by the markets is analyst expectations. If the earnings of the company exceed the predictions made by major analysts prior to the earnings call, this usually results in jubilation and rising stock prices. In many cases, the stock can rise 10-20% in value overnight.

Of course, companies often disappoint. In fact, it doesn't even matter if a company reports a profit, if they fail to meet the expectations of the market, this can lead to a crash in the stock share price. Movements in price can be as large as movements due to positive earnings reports. If the reports are actually bad, that is, they not only fail to meet expectations but also report a loss or some other negative news. This can lead to massive losses on the stock. This happened to Netflix and Tesla in recent earnings calls. Netflix reported a loss of subscribers, which caused a plunge in their stock price.

A strangle is a two-leg strategy, which is just another way of saying that we will use two different options to create the trade. Strangles are speculative trades, and therefore, we will buy to open these positions.

You might be asking how we can profit no matter which way the stock moves. The answer is that a strangle involves buying a call option and a put option simultaneously on the same stock. They will have the same expiration dates but different strike prices. The movement of the stock has to be large enough to exceed the cost of buying both options. If the stock price rises, this means that the Put Option which is a part of our trade, is going to expire worthless. If the stock price crashes, on the other hand, that means that the call option is going to expire worthless.

For our breakeven price, we need to take into account the total cost of entering into the position, so it will be the cost of the call option + the cost of the put option. So, if the stock were to break to the upside, the price would have to rise above the strike price of the call option + total cost of buying both options. If the strike price were $100 and we paid $3 for the call option and $2 for the put option, then the price of the stock would have to go above $100 + $3 + 2 = $105 before we can make a profit.

To figure out the breakeven point for the put option, we start with the strike price used for the put option and then subtract the total cost for entering the position. Therefore, if our strike price for the put option on this hypothetical trade were $90, the breakeven point to the downside would just be $90 - $3 - $2 = $85.

In this hypothetical setup, we would not make any profit if the share price were to stay within the two strike prices. Specifically, this means that if the share price stayed between $90 and $100, we would lose on the trade. The total loss would be equal to the cost of the two options, or $3 + 42 = $5. Since there are 100 shares underlying the option, the total loss would be $5 x 100 = $500. The maximum loss occurs if the share price stays the same. Of course, the probability of a share price staying the same after an earnings call is practically nil. The stock is going to move somewhat, so the question is: will the stock price move enough so that you make a profit? If it doesn't, any movement in the share price will at least reduce your losses.

So how much can you make? To the upside, in theory, the maximum gain is unlimited. It depends on how high the stock price rises. Share prices on big stocks can rise $30 or $40 after an earnings call, and so it is possible to make thousands of dollars in profit. Of course, that doesn't mean you should go into these types of trades expecting that kind of profit. However, it is possible to earn substantial profits.

To the downside, the maximum gain is equal to the share price when you enter the position multiplied by 100. To earn the maximum gain to the downside, the share price would have to drop all the way down to zero. Of course, that is something that rarely happens, so don't expect it. But it is not uncommon to see share prices on big stocks drop $20, $30, or $40 a share after a bad earnings call. So, to the downside, very large profits are also possible.

# How to Implement the Strategy

When there are big events like earnings calls, stock prices can even change dramatically after hours before the markets open the next morning. Therefore, it is important to plan ahead for using this type of strategy.

The first step is to identify an event that is coming up where the strategy might be appropriate. For stocks, the earnings call is the primary event to look for. Therefore, find stocks you are interested in and look up the dates of their upcoming earnings calls. These occur on a quarterly basis; therefore, we have four opportunities per year for each stock to employ the strategy.

Another opportunity might be the upcoming company announcements. For example, Apple has regular presentations it gives every year. They have a developer conference where the new operating system for the iPhone and iPad devices is unveiled to the public for the first time. This may or may not have a big impact on the viewpoint of major market analysts, and so it could cause a large shift in share prices of Apple if the changes to the operating system are viewed as having a possible impact on Apple's future bottom line. In the fall, Apple has presentations where they reveal their latest iPhones and changes to their computer line. If there are major changes and announcements by Apple, this can have a big impact on stock prices as well.

Apple is the quintessential example for using the strategy in this manner, but you can look up and follow different companies to see when and if they are going to make major announcements about their product line, or if there are going to be upcoming announcements on things that might impact the company's fortunes. For example, a pharmaceutical company might be seeking FDA approval for a major drug. If the drug is approved, the stock of the company could shoot up significantly. If the drug is rejected, the stock could decline by a large amount. This possibility suggests that a strangle might be an appropriate technique to use in order to earn profits from these events.

Index funds are also possible targets for the strategy. Any index fund on the blue-chip companies can be considered, most notably the S & P 500. You can also consider index funds on the Dow Jones Industrial Average, the NASDAQ 100, or the total market. In this case, major news events and releases of economic data will be important to consider. Of course, it is hard, if not impossible, to plan for unexpected events. But there are major scheduled events that occur on a monthly and quarterly basis. These include announcements of interest rate changes by the federal reserve, announcements on jobs and the unemployment rate, and announcements of the GDP growth rate.

Just like with stocks, the actual nature of the announcements may not be what drives changes in the share prices of index funds. Rather, it will be how the announcement compares to the expectations held by the market. For example, if the market expects the creation of 170,000 jobs, but it's announced that there were 190,000 jobs created, the market will be jubilant. This would mean that index funds like SPY would see large spikes in share price.

Once you have an event identified, you can buy one or more strangle contracts on the stock or index fund in question. A strangle is entered into as a single transaction, and so you will buy the call and put option simultaneously. Remember that options have time decay. This can mean that buying a strangle far ahead of time can be overly expensive. This can mean that some balance is going to be necessary. It is advisable that you get some experience trading straight call and put options for a few months before attempting this. As you are doing so, you should be studying the market behaviors and look at the prices of strangles on your trading platform to see how they change with time. In particular, look for earnings calls and see what happens.

The balance is going to come from the anticipation of the markets. Since people know that big movements in share price are possible when earnings calls are approaching, although the options have time decay, prices are going to be rising from increasing demand.

So, it is a matter of balance, is there enough increasing demand to wipe out the time decay. The longer you wait to get into a position the more it is going to cost if there is a lot of interest swirling around the stock. This can happen with major stocks like Tesla, Facebook, Apple, and so on.

Once you've gotten in your position, you have to be ready to sell it at the right moment. Typically (but not always), what happens in these situations is that stock prices are going to rise very quickly. Companies may have a late afternoon earnings call. They often schedule these such that they take place after the markets close. Even though the markets are closed, there will be after-hours trading. Under normal circumstances, after-hours trading doesn't have significant impacts, but after earnings call, the impacts can be dramatic. Prices on a stock might rise or fall 20-30% even before the next market open.

What happens next is hard to say, as the market is inherently unpredictable. If there is going to be more movement, it is likely to occur in the first 30 minutes after the market open. At some point, the stock may stabilize at new levels of support and resistance. How quickly it does this will depend on the intensity of the earnings call. If the earnings call only mildly exceeded or failed to meet expectations, then the stock price might settle at a new level fairly quickly. If the announcement was dramatic, then a sell off or rush to buy the stock might last for a longer time period.

If you decide to implement the strategy, you should be prepared to be paying close attention to the market the morning after the earnings call or other announcement. Be ready to sell your position so that you can take an acceptable level of profit before the market stabilizes, and the demand for strangles on the stock starts to decline. The key here is to take advantage of latecomers to the marketplace. There are always people that come in late, but they eventually fizzle. However, buyers will come in late after noticing the large shift in share prices for the stock, and they will be interested in buying up strangles so that they can profit from any late hour movements in share price. But the key to being a successful options trader is to not be one of those late arrivals. You should plan these trades out and already be in your position before the earnings call. Remember, with a strangle you are going to be earning profit no matter which direction the stock moves, so if it goes up or down is not going to be your concern. The chart below graphically illustrates the way a strangle works.

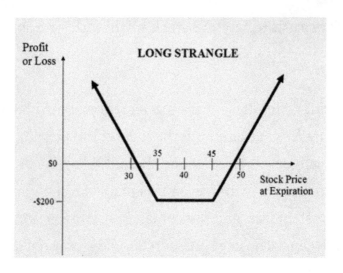

In the center of the chart, you see a flat line. This is the range in between the strike prices where you will have maximum loss. From here, on both sides, the line slopes upward to the breakeven point, which remember is the strike price + cost to enter the position on the upside, and the strike price minus the cost to enter the position on the downside. From there, the more the price moves past the strike prices of the options used to set up the position, the more profit that is earned. In the graph above, we see a hypothetical example with strike prices of $35 and $45, with a total cost to enter the position of around $5. The chart is for illustration purposes only and does not represent actual prices.

Let's look at a real example to see how much this would cost. Facebook is trading at $208 a share, and we can enter a strangle that expires in one week for a price of $2.10, or $210 in total. The strangle has strike prices of $212.50 for the call and $205 for the put.

The breakeven point for the upside is $214.60. This is computed by adding the cost to enter the position, which is $2.10, to the strike price of $212.50. To earn a profit with this trade, the share price of Facebook would have to rise above $214.50. If the share price rose to $216.50, you would earn a $190 profit. If it rose to $224, you could earn around $1,000 in profit.

Under normal conditions, you wouldn't expect the stock price of Facebook to rise to $224 a share. But if there was a very good earnings call, that is something that is definitely in the realm of possibility.

On the downside, the maximum possible profit on this trade is $20,200. To be profitable, it would have to drop below the strike price used for the put option, which is $205, less the cost of entering the position, which is $2.10, and so the breakeven point is $202.90. If there was a bad earnings call and the share price were to drop to $195 or so, you could earn a profit of $750.

Once the event has occurred, you can risk holding the position to expiration. If there are no other major movements in the share price, the options will expire, and you'll earn your profits. But a good strategy is to simply sell the position for a profit once the major movement in stock prices has occurred.

## Straddle

Now we turn our attention to a related strategy that is called a straddle. This is also a two-legged strategy that is designed to take advantage of price breakouts of a stock, without regard to the direction that the breakout occurs. Like a strangle, a straddle will also involve buying a call option and a put option on the same stock, and with the same expiration date, simultaneously.

However, a straddle differs from a strangle in one key aspect. To set up a straddle, you will also set up the trade so that the call option and the put have the same expiration date. The chart for a straddle is shown below. This narrows down the range over which there are losses. Maximum loss on the trade would occur if the stock price were equal to the strike price at option expiration.

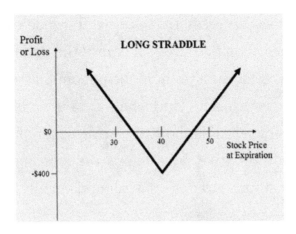

To summarize, both a strangle, and a straddle is set up in order to earn profit from large moves in the price of a stock. In either case, it doesn't matter if the stock moves up or down in price. No matter what direction the stock moves, they will earn a profit provided that the price move is large enough to overcome the breakeven points. Like a strangle, you can use straddles when there are big events or announcements coming up, such as earnings calls.

The same type of strategies should be employed when using straddles rather than strangles. This means that you want to enter your position over a time frame of a week up to maybe three or four weeks prior to a big event like an earnings call. Over the time period between your purchase and the earnings call, the straddle will gain in value from stock movements, regardless of whether or not the price of the stock moves up or it moves down. If the price of the stock increases, the value of the straddle will increase because of the call option that is a part of the trade. However, it could also lose value as a result of the put option that is a part of the trade. The price has to move one way or the other so that the share price is higher than the strike price + cost of the position, or lower than the strike price minus the cost of the position. Remember that for a straddle, the call option and the put option both have the same strike prices.

Let's say that the price of some stock is $234 per share. We create a straddle with a strike price of $235 a share. Although maximum loss occurs when the strike price is equal to the share price, we want to pick a strike price that meets that condition when entering the trade, because we are doing so expecting the share price to move off the strike price in one direction or the other at a later date before the options expire.

For our example, we are entering the trade 21 days before expiration. At this point, the call is $6.93, and the put is $7.89, and so the total cost to enter the position would be $14.92. Let's say that there is an earnings call when the option is five days to expiration.

Now, by 15 days to expiration, in anticipation of the upcoming earnings call, the share price might have moved a bit. Let's suppose that the market is expecting a good earnings call, and so share prices are going up. If the share price went up to $237, this is a modest gain that, despite time decay, will help the value of the call option. It has risen from $6.93 to $7.36. However, the put option has lost some value due to time decay combined with the modestly higher stock price, and it's now going for $5.33.

Our plan, however, is to hold the position until the earnings call. Remember that earnings call also impact volatility. We are setting the implied volatility at 33% for this exercise, but as we get closer to the earnings call, that value will rise.

Now 10 days to expiration, which would be five days to the earnings call in our scenario. The share price has risen to $240 share since the markets are expecting good news. Implied volatility has also increased to 37%. At this point, the call has jumped to $8.37, but the put is now down to $3.63.

Moving forward to just 7 days to expiration, there are only two days left until the earnings call. Now implied volatility has risen to 45%. The share price has increased steadily with the passing days and now stands at $245. Under these conditions, the call is $12.26, and the put is $2.25. The total value now is $14.51, and it cost $14.92 to enter the position, so we have a mild loss at this point – but it should be ignored. We need to hold the position until the earnings call.

Later that day, the stock is at $247, and the implied volatility has risen to 50%. The call is now $14.32, and the put is $2.30, so our position is now worth $16.62. Since it cost $14.92 to enter the position, we are now at a point of profitability to the tune of $16.62 - $14.92 = $1.70. If you wanted to, you could sell it now for a profit of $170. You'd find an eager buyer without a doubt because most traders would be anxious to get in on the trade prior to the actual earnings call.

Finally, we reach the earnings call. It beats expectations by a surprising margin, and the price of the stock jumps $23 a share in after-hours trading. At market open, the call option is worth $36.01, and the and the put is worth pennies on the dollar. At this point, the put option is worthless, but the call option has gone up so much in value that we are looking at a profit of $36.01 - $14.92 = $21.09 per share, putting us in a position where we can sell for a total profit of $2,109.

If the stock continued climbing the morning after the earnings call, which sometimes happens, we could earn even more profits. If it went to $280 a share by the afternoon, the call option would be worth $45. In that case, we'd have another $900 in total profits on the trade. Of course, you are taking some risk. The longer you hold the position. The stock might start declining a bit or stop rising. And if you hold it overnight, you are going to get hit with time decay. The put option is entirely worthless at this point, but it really doesn't matter.

Suppose that instead, the price had plummeted. Our hypothetical company might have missed expectations by a large margin, and rather than rising by a huge amount, it could drop to $210 a share instead. The beauty of the straddle is that in this scenario, we make a profit as well. This time, the call option would be completely worthless on the trading day after the earnings call, but the put option would be worth $24.99, giving us about a $1,000 profit. The more the stock drops, the more profit we would earn. The same holds true for a strangle but remember with the strangle the call and put options have different strike prices, and there might be a wider range over which the stock needs to move in order to earn profits. But in either case, the goals are the same.

## Tips and Things to Watch Out For

There are a few things to watch out for with the strangle and straddle. For a strangle, you probably want to bracket the strike prices of your call and put such that the current share price is in the middle. For a straddle, you can use the current share price as your strike or pick a strike price that is very close to the current share price.

You can enter the position at any time, but depending on market conditions, costs might go up a lot in the days coming up to the earnings call. Prior to making your first trade, it is a good idea to simply watch from the sidelines and wait until the next quarter before actually doing trades. In fact, many trading platforms have demo accounts that let you go through the process of making trades, but without spending any money. In other words, they are pretending, simulated trades, but using the real data going on in the marketplace. New traders are often quite anxious and want to get in on the action, but it is worth spending one quarter going through the practice trades to get some experience doing it without risking real money. Since you are just observing, you can also keep an eye on multiple stocks to see how they and options prices are changing as their earnings date approaches, since all the major stocks are going to be doing earnings calls within a couple of weeks of each other.

Another thing to consider is liquidity, an issue that we've raised before. The bottom line here is that once the large shift in share price has occurred, you want to be able to get out of your position quickly. For this reason, you really need to focus on high volume, popular stocks if you are going to employ this strategy. So, you'll be checking the open interest and volume. It's good to focus on the big-name movers such as Amazon, Netflix, Facebook, Google, and Apple, the so-called FAANGS, at least as a beginner. These are not cheap stocks, of course, and that cuts both ways. It is more expensive to enter a position, but the potential profits are also quite large. These are the stocks that will experience very big moves in share price based on earnings calls, and they are also highly liquid and so you will have no problem selling a position when you need to.

For practice without risking money, you can try the technique out on lower priced stocks like AMD, which is trading at around $45 a share. We can enter a straddle on AMD for about $345. Apple is trading at $297 a share. A straddle choosing the closest strike price to the share price would cost $1,448. The Apple straddle is likely to earn far higher profits if the stocks moved a given percentage, so there are tradeoffs that have to be made. Of course, in the beginning, you are probably not going to want to risk large amounts of capital.

# Chapter 7: Call and Put Spreads (Vertical Spreads)

In this chapter, we are going to discuss an advanced technique that can be used to speculate on stock price movements or as a method of generating regular income selling options. These techniques are called vertical spreads because they involve trading two options simultaneously of the same type which have a spread in strike prices, but the same expiration dates. There are two ways that you can set these trades up. They are going to involve two options of the same type. The trades also involving buying one option and selling another option with a different strike price, but the same expiration date, and of course, on the same underlying stock.

If you spend more on the option that you buy than you do on the option that you sell, this is going to create a net debit. The purpose of a debit spread is to trade on speculation as you would trading a single option. So, for example, if you thought that the stock price would go up, you'd buy a call option and sell a call option. This procedure will actually reduce your risk as opposed to buying a single call option. But the tradeoff of reducing your risk in this fashion is that you will cap the amount of profit you can make. For a single call option, the amount of possible profit you can earn is theoretically unlimited.

Keep in mind the jargon used in spreads by the industry. An option that you sell is short, while an option that you buy is long.

## Debit Spreads

A debit spread is the purchase of one option and the sale of another option of the same type and with the same expiration date with different strike prices, such that the complete transaction results in a net debit. There are two types of debit spreads. You can do a call debit spread, which means buying a call and selling a call, or you can do a put debit spread, which means buying a put and selling a put simultaneously. The purpose of a debit spread is to reduce the amount of risk you face if the trade does not work, but this comes at the expense of capping profits below what you would get with an equivalent winning trade just buying a call or a put.

Let's consider the situation involving calls first. A call debit spread is also known as a bull debit spread or a bull call spread. The reason for the terminology is that this is a trade that you would enter into if you were bullish on the stock. In other words, you're expecting the share price of the stock to increase by the time the options expire.

This is a two-legged trade, meaning that we are going to trade two options simultaneously. The two options will have different strike prices, but the same expiration dates. This makes the trade a vertical spread, the vertical being along the strike prices. For a call debit spread, you are going to buy a call option with a lower strike price and sell an out of the money call option with a higher strike price.

Entering into this type of spread is going to change the Greeks associated with a position, as compared to simply buying a call option at a given strike price. It will reduce the delta and theta for the trade. This means that with a smaller delta, your position is going to be impacted less by changes in the underlying stock price. But that really isn't a concern. There is still enough delta that the trade can be profitable. Our position is also less sensitive to theta, which means it will be a little less sensitive to time decay as far as losing value. But don't rest on your laurels, any option position that you enter with a net debt (aka buying to enter the position) is impacted by time decay, and a call debit spread is no exception.

In order to make a profit, we need the underlying stock price to appreciate in value. The maximum profit that you can earn on a call debit spread is as follows:

Max profit = difference in strike prices − premium paid to enter the position

Looking at Apple, here are a couple of examples. We could enter into a call debit spread using two out of the money options by buying the $302.50 strike price and selling the $307.50 strike price. The cost to enter this position with one week to expiration is $1.19. The width of the strike prices is:

$307.50 - $302.50 = $5

Therefore, the maximum profit is found by subtracting the cost to enter the position from this value:

$5 - $1.19 = $3.81

Once again, there are 100 underlying shares, so it would cost $119 to enter the position and we could earn $381. Again, this is a capped amount. Maximum profit occurs if the share price goes above the strike price of the call option that we sell (the short call) in order to enter the position. If you had only bought a put option, your possible profits could be much higher. No matter how much higher the stock price goes above the strike price of the short option, your profit stays the same at a fixed amount. So, any time you enter into a call debit spread, if the share price of the underlying stock goes above the short strike price, sell the position to get out of it with your profits. If conditions warrant it, you can just let the options expire.

Maximum losses for a call debit spread are capped. The maximum loss that you can incur with a call debit spread is when the underlying stock price drops below the long strike price (that is the strike price of the option that you buy to enter into the position). Again, this is a fixed value. So, no matter how low the price of the underlying stock drops, even if it were to drop all the way to zero, the number of losses that you could incur would be limited to the premium paid to enter the position.

The breakeven point occurs at the strike price of the long call plus the premium paid to enter the position. Using the Apple example, the premium paid was $1.19, and the lower strike price (or the strike price of the long call) was $302.50. So, the breakeven point is $302.50 + $1.19 = $303.69. Let's summarize this for our example, and this will help you understand how these trades work:

- If the stock drops below $302.50, even by a penny, we incur the maximum loss. That is the premium paid to enter the position, which in this case would be $1.19 per share or $119 for the 100 shares in total.

- The breakeven point is $302.50 + $1.19 = $303.69. If the stock is between $302.50 and $303.69, we incur losses, but they will be less than the total premium paid. If it reaches $303.69, we neither lose nor earn money.

- In between $303.69 and the short strike price of $307.50, we would earn a small profit.

- If the underlying share price were to go above $307.50, then we'd earn a maximum profit of $381. Even if the share price were to go up to $500, it wouldn't matter, our profit is strictly capped in this trade.

A call debit spread is a smarter way to play rising stock prices as opposed to buying call options. You actually cut your risk, because when you sell a call option, you get paid premium for that call option. Since the strike price is higher than the strike price for the long call in this trade, the amount you get paid is lower than the amount spent to buy the long call. However, it reduces the amount you have to pay, as compared to buying the long call by itself.

## Put Debit Spreads

Now let's consider a put debit spread. This trade also goes by the name of bear debit spread or bear put spread. The purpose of this trade is the same goal as you would have to buy a single put option; you are anticipating that the share price of the underlying stock is going to go down. The basic setup is the same as it is with a call debit spread. However, since we are looking at put options, we are going to be doing the reverse in our thinking. We will belong on a higher strike price and short on a lower strike price. Both put options that are a part of the trade are going to have the same expiration date.

Once again, the maximum profit will be the width of the strike prices minus the cost to enter the position. The maximum loss you can incur on the trade is the premium paid to enter the position.

From here, things are just reversed in the sense that we are looking for declining prices in the share price of the underlying stock. Therefore, the maximum profit is going to occur if the share price of the underlying stock goes below the strike price of the short put option. The breakeven point will be the strike price of the long-put option minus the premium paid to enter the position. Again, the long-put option will have a higher strike price than the short put option in this case. This is a strategy that can be employed to minimize risk when you believe that the share price of the underlying stock is going to decline.

Debit spreads are limited risk, limited reward strategies. They are set up in order to reduce the amount of risk (the amount of money you can lose) associated with a trade. The cost of doing this is that you also have a reduced profit potential for the trade. However, a lesson you should learn is that very few professional options traders just do straight trading of call and put options. That type of strategy is a high-risk strategy. But you can do the same type of speculating using debit spreads.

## Put Credit Spreads

Now let's continue our investigation of vertical spreads but shift gears. This time we are going to talk about using options in order to generate income, rather than speculating on the direction of the stock. Of course, there is always a little bit of speculation, but in this case, we are only hoping that the price stays above a certain value, and not worry about what it is doing otherwise.

A put credit spread is created by trading two put options simultaneously. It can be said that this is set up just like the put debit spread, but we reverse the roles of which option is bought or sold. In this case, we are going to sell a put option with a higher strike price. The purpose of doing so is to generate a credit to our account that earns income. In order to reduce our overall risk of the trade, we are going to sell a put option with a lower strike price. A put option with a higher strike price is going to cost more than a put option with a lower strike price; therefore, there is a net credit on the trade.

There is only one rule to use when deciding to trade put credit spreads. You want to trade put credit spreads in good markets. It doesn't have to be a particularly strong bull market; it just has to be a market where prices are not declining. This applies to the individual stock as well, so you want to trade put credit spreads when the stock is doing well. A good rule of thumb is to avoid trading put credit spreads during the week of an earnings call when stock prices might suddenly plummet.

The main thing to learn about put credit spreads is that this is a selling position. You are going to sell to open, and therefore you will have the obligations of a seller associated with the short put with the higher strike price. That is, you could be "assigned". When a put option is exercised, the buyer will sell you 100 shares of stock at the strike price, no matter what the market price is. And theoretically, you need to have the cash on hand to cover the transaction. When you are assigned, you are required by law to buy the 100 shares.

But the good news about the put credit spread is you don't actually have to buy the shares, and your liability is capped. The reason is that you have covered yourself by purchasing a put option with a lower strike price. What happens is you are able to exercise the put option with the lower strike price. It works like this – you have to buy the 100 shares at the higher strike price. But you can turn around and sell them at the lower strike price by exercising the other put option. So, with a credit spread, you are assigned on one option and can exercise the other option. You would lose money in this situation; it would be the difference between the strike prices minus the net credit received. But at least it is a fixed amount of money.

In practice, you aren't going to have to do anything at all, because your broker takes care of all this automatically in the event the option expires in a situation where it could be exercised. As a trader, you won't know all this happened, the stocks will be bought and sold on your behalf, and you will only see the end result.

In order to sell put options, you are going to need some collateral. This is done by putting a cash deposit into your account. The purpose of doing so is to cover the theoretical loss that can occur if the trade does not work out for you. To see how this works, let's look at an example.

Consider a put credit spread on Apple that expires in one week. The strike prices are $297.50 and $295. The breakeven price is the strike price of the short put option, $297.50, less the net credit received. It is important to remember that with a credit spread, you don't actually pay anything to enter the position. You are actually receiving credit for it. But you won't actually see the credit materialize until the options expire or you buy it back.

In this case, the credit received is $1.12 per share, or $100. So, the breakeven point is $296.38. As long as the stock price stays above $296.38, you will make a profit (at the time of writing, it's $297.35). Maximum gain happens if the stock price stays or goes above the upper strike price. So, if it stays at or goes above $297.50 per share, a real possibility in this case, then you would earn the maximum credit of $112. Maximum loss is computed by taking the difference between the strike prices and subtracting the credit received. In this case, we have ($297.50 - $295) - $1.12 = $1.38, or $138.

In order to actually enter the trade, you would have to deposit some cash to cover that potential loss.

Put credit spreads are popular for generating regular income. Many professional options traders earn a living by selling put credit spreads at regular intervals. You can sell as many as you can back with collateral and can mix it up by using different stocks. The higher the share price on a stock, the more you can earn by selling put credit spreads. And at all times, the possible losses you can incur are known and fixed.

# Call Credit Spreads

Put credit spreads sound great, but of course, the stock market is not going up and up all the time, even though it seems that way right now because we've been in a long-time bull market. What to do then? The answer is simple – you switch to selling call credit spreads in a bear market or when a stock is crashing. A call credit spread is designed to earn money when stock prices are dropping or staying below the lower strike price used in the spread.

In the call debit spread, we trade two call options with the same expiration date, and that is what we are going to be doing in this case. With the call debit spread, we bought a call option with a lower strike price and sold a call option with a higher strike price. Since call options with lower strike prices are worth more money, this results in a net debit to our account.

Now, we are going to do the reverse. So, we are going to sell a call option with a low strike price, and then buy one with a high strike price to reduce our risk. This will result in a net credit to our account. Other than the differences in the relationships of the strike prices and the fact these are calls rather than puts, the principles are exactly the same as a put credit spread.

In this case, the risk of assignment is that we would have to sell shares. But when using a credit spread, you don't actually have to own the shares. When a call option is exercised, the seller/writer of the option is required to sell 100 shares of stock at the strike price. In this case, if that were to happen to you with a spread, you don't have to do anything other than cry when you get your losses. The broker will sell the shares on your behalf and exercise the long option to recoup some of the losses.

If you decide to be an options seller, you can make a good living switching between call and put credit spreads as market conditions warrant. This is completely different than stock trading, as you will never have to worry about whether the stock market is bearish or bullish, you can earn money under any circumstances using these methods.

## Time Decay and Buy Backs

Two things work in your favor as an options seller. For options buyers, time decay works against them because the option is losing value. As an options seller, that doesn't affect you – in fact, it helps you a great deal if you are selling out of the money options (and they stay out of the money). As a seller, time decay works in your favor as the options become less valuable to buyers. That makes it less likely they are going to be exercised as time passes.

The second key strategy is to buy your positions back either close to expiration, or in the event, they go in the money. If the options are not close to expiration, but they go in the money, there is a chance that they would be exercised. However, that is generally less likely. But if you feel there is a risk that the options are not going to go out of the money again prior to expiration, you can simply buy the contract back. When you buy an options contract back, you are freed of all obligations associated with that contract.

# Chapter 8: Selling Options

In the last chapter, we actually touched on selling options, doing it by mitigating risk using credit spreads. In this case, we are going to talk about selling options without mitigating the risk, which is simply selling them alone. If the options are backed, we have covered calls and cash covered puts. If the options are not backed by anything, they are called "naked". Although it sounds crazy to sell naked options at first glance, the truth is many professional options traders make $500,000 and up per year selling naked options. Let's investigate each of these in turn in this chapter.

## Covered Calls

The least risky option strategy is to sell covered calls. In order to sell a covered call, you must own 100 shares of stock. Many investors earn income from dividends, and covered calls provide an alternative and often more lucrative way to earn money from stock ownership. However, it does carry some risk in that your stock may be "called away". That is, if the stock price moves above the strike price of any option you sell + the premium received for the option, the buyer of the option may choose to exercise it, which means they have the legal right to buy 100 shares of stock from you at the strike price.

But, if you own 1,000 shares in Apple (actually any number of a specific stock of 100 shares or more), or some other good company that can fetch a good options premium, and you are willing to assume the risk of having your stock called away, this can be used to generate regular income from your stocks. Each option that you sell must be backed by 100 shares of stock.

When you sell an option, you get to keep the premium that is paid for the option. In fact, you can keep it no matter what happens. So that is cash in your pocket even if you have to sell the shares. And in many cases, you aren't going to lose anything in a fundamental sense. If you had purchased the shares in the past at a lower price, this means that you will actually be selling them at a profit, although the amount of profit you earn will be lower than what you could have earned on the stock market. That is because you will have to sell them at the strike price, no matter how high the stock price rises. But there is the possibility that you can still "lose" in the trade and come out financially ahead.

Different people have different risk tolerance, and for some people, this is going to be too much. They aren't going to be willing to risk losing their stock. But if you are willing to take on that risk, there are ways to minimize it. Although you will make less money, you can sell out of the money call options that have a low probability of being exercised. Suppose that we had 300 shares of Tesla stock. It is currently trading at $441.91 per share. We could sell a call option with a $450 strike price to receive a premium of $14.93 per share. This option is listed by the broker as having a 70% chance of profit. For 100 shares, that would be $1,493. If we did that for all 300 shares, the total premium received would be $4,479. So, you could make big money doing this.

Like with credit spreads, you can always buy your options back. In the situation where you sell a covered call and then buy it back later, you are freed of the obligation of having to sell your shares, and you get to keep your shares. So generally speaking, unless you are careless, it is a low-risk strategy. Keep in mind that if the option goes in the money, there is a chance that a buyer can exercise it and require you to sell the shares. But most options are not exercised until expiration. So, you can avoid the situation by selling in the money options prior to expiration.

## Cash Protected Puts

Another way to sell single options is by selling cash protected puts. A cash protected put means that you deposit the money in your brokerage account that would be necessary to buy 100 shares of stock. This is a less popular strategy for a few reasons. If you have that kind of money lying around, there are better ways to utilize it in stock and options trading. Another reason is that you can sell put credit spreads and only tie up a small fraction of the capital.

This can be an expensive proposition. To sell the $437.50 put on Tesla expiring in one week, you would need to deposit $42,982.34 into your brokerage account. For the trouble, you would make $750. That would only be a 1.7% return on your money. If you have $42k to invest, I am sure you don't want to tie it up to make $750, especially when you could sell put credit spreads and make $750 tying up, maybe $1,200 or so.

The bottom line is that cash protected puts are not a favored strategy. In fact, they might be called pointless.

## Naked Put Options

Finally, we come to the holy grail of income generation using options, which is selling naked options. This is a simpler strategy than selling vertical spreads, but the goals are the same. We have simply removed the risk mitigating factor. When you sell naked put options, you are selling one option in each trade. You receive the premium credit, and that's it.

In order to sell naked options, you are required to have a margin account and to deposit a certain amount of money to cover a trade. The amount of money is a fraction of the amount of money that you have to put in in order to sell a cash protected put. So, while you might be required to deposit $180,000 to sell cash protected puts against Amazon, you'd only have to deposit around $11,000 to sell naked Amazon puts.

The biggest risk of naked put options is assignment. That is, you are not paying attention, and the share price drops well below your strike price, and someone exercises the option. That would put you in a position of having to buy the shares. Then you could resell them on the market at the lower share price and take the loss.

This is why a margin account is necessary. A margin account is a type of account that lets you borrow money and shares from the broker. So, the required capital you must deposit helps cover your losses to some extent. You are going to have to borrow from the broker to buy the shares, and then after you sell them on the market the collateral you put up will cover the net loss.

You can also sell naked call options when stock market prices are declining. These are well-known winning strategies used by professionals. In the event that it looks like it is a losing trade, you use the same techniques you would use for credit spreads, that is you simply buy back the contracts.

# Chapter 9: Tips for Successful Trading

In this chapter, we are going to run through some tips for successful options trading. These tips are based on years of experience trading options and come from many different people.

## Set Stops on Your Trades

The biggest risk for an options trader is that they will get emotional during a trade. This can result in selling too early because of panic about declining options prices or staying in a trade too long because of greed. To avoid these problems, you can set a rule on the amount of loss you are willing to accept and the amount of profit you are willing to take on a trade. Many brokers allow you to hard code this with the trading software so that it gets implemented automatically. Then you don't have to worry about your trades. You just accept the end results. Another way to say this is to have a defined exit plan.

## Letting Options Expire

Never let options expire, unless specific conditions are met. If you are buying call options and want to actually own the stock, then you can let an in the money option expire. If you are trading out of the money options, you should never let them expire. Sell them even it would mean a losing trade, a day or two before expiration. That way you can at least cut your losses.

## Consider Rolling Out Trades That Aren't Working

Rolling out an option means closing the position and then entering the position again, but with a longer expiration date. This gives you more time to work the trade by pushing the expiration date to the future.

## Avoid Options with Low Volume

Remember, you always want to look for liquidity. One of the biggest mistakes made by novice options traders is to trade options that are illiquid. Remember the rule for open interest, only trade options that have an open interest of 100 or higher. That will save you from getting into trouble trading options with low volume where you could get stuck in a trade.

## Attempting to Make up for Past Failures

Don't try to trade using a higher volume in order to make up for past mistakes.

# Conclusion

Thank you for making it through to the end of *Options Trading Crash Course*, let's hope it was informative and able to provide you with all of the tools you need to achieve your goals whatever they may be.

Options trading is a very exciting part of the stock market. With options trading, you can control large amounts of stock without actually owning it. This means that you can earn profits from movements in the stock price without risking huge amounts of capital. The return on investment on options is simply much better than the possible return on investment that you can earn trading options.

In this book, I have attempted to demystify options trading for you. We have explained what an option is, the difference between call and put options, and the strategies used by professional options traders when investing in options.

My hope is that rather than join the scare chorus that surrounds options from "financial advisors", I have shown you that options are actually a rational investment that can help you build your own successful trading business. Whether you engage in "speculation" or trading for investment income, options can help you read a six or even seven-figure income from your trading business, provided that you make careful trades and stick to the fundamental principles that are guaranteed to lead to success.

Your next steps are to actually get your feet wet with some trades. Start slowly, and spend some time trading small numbers of call and put options to build up some experience. Be sure to do both. Many novice traders are scared away from put options because they are not used to thinking in terms of earning money from declining stock prices. So, it's important to get over that and actually go through the experience of earning money while the company is having losses.

From there, you can start to employ options strategies after you've got a few months of experience making some trades. Before settling on a favorite, try the different strategies to see what you like best. Some people will end up focusing on only one trade. For example, many professional traders only trade iron condors, while others only sell put options. Others have a lot of variety and will engage in whatever trades suit them at the moment and what the market conditions are. This is a matter of personal taste, so you will have to figure out what works best for you.

I want to wish my readers good luck in the trading business!

Finally, if you found this book useful in any way, a review on Amazon is always appreciated!

CPSIA information can be obtained
at www.ICGtesting.com
Printed in the USA
BVHW052248070421
604338BV00007B/611

9 781801 942751